Cambridge Elements ≡

Elements in the Philosophy of Friedrich Nietzsche
edited by
Kaitlyn Creasy
California State University, San Bernardino
Matthew Meyer
The University of Scranton

NIETZSCHE ON VIRTUE

Mark Alfano
Macquarie University, Sydney

CAMBRIDGE
UNIVERSITY PRESS

Shaftesbury Road, Cambridge CB2 8EA, United Kingdom

One Liberty Plaza, 20th Floor, New York, NY 10006, USA

477 Williamstown Road, Port Melbourne, VIC 3207, Australia

314–321, 3rd Floor, Plot 3, Splendor Forum, Jasola District Centre,
New Delhi – 110025, India

103 Penang Road, #05–06/07, Visioncrest Commercial, Singapore 238467

Cambridge University Press is part of Cambridge University Press & Assessment,
a department of the University of Cambridge.

We share the University's mission to contribute to society through the pursuit of
education, learning and research at the highest international levels of excellence.

www.cambridge.org
Information on this title: www.cambridge.org/9781009517386

DOI: 10.1017/9781009417402

First published 2024

A catalogue record for this publication is available from the British Library

ISBN 978-1-009-51738-6 Hardback
ISBN 978-1-009-41737-2 Paperback
ISSN 2976-5722 (online)
ISSN 2976-5714 (print)

Nietzsche on Virtue

Elements in the Philosophy of Friedrich Nietzsche

DOI: 10.1017/9781009417402
First published online: December 2024

Mark Alfano
Macquarie University, Sydney

Author for correspondence: Mark Alfano, mark.alfano@gmail.com

Abstract: The author argues for an interpretation of Nietzsche on virtue according to which Nietzsche believes that because different people have different constellations of instincts and other drives, and because instincts and drives can only be shaped and redirected within boundaries, he recommends different virtues as fitting and conducive to flourishing for different types of people. In his own type, these include curiosity, intellectual courage, the pathos of distance, having a sense of humor, and solitude. This interpretation is supported by both a digital humanities methodology and close readings of passages from Nietzsche's middle, mature, and late works.

Keywords: Nietzsche, virtue, drive, curiosity, intellectual courage

ISBNs: 9781009517386 (HB), 9781009417372 (PB), 9781009417402 (OC)
ISSNs: 2976-5722 (online), 2976-5714 (print)

Contents

What Satan had for sale in the garden was knowledge.
—Cormac McCarthy, *Stella Maris*

1 Introduction

Nietzsche is an idiosyncratic philosopher, and the virtues he elaborates and celebrates in his books are equally idiosyncratic. While most philosophers offer universal theories of virtue, with perhaps some wiggle room to fine-tune dispositions to individual natures, Nietzsche insists that different virtues are fitting for different types of people. In *Nicomachean Ethics* 1106b, Aristotle articulates the doctrine of the golden mean in a way that allows for different people to manifest the same virtue in different ways. But he does not suggest that different virtues are appropriate for different people, except for a few stray remarks about gender and class. By contrast, Nietzsche thinks that someone's type determines which virtues it would be fitting for them to cultivate. He thinks some types are embodied by many of us, the "herd" type being the most numerous and the "last man" a harbinger of potential future homogenization. But he also thinks that some types are relatively rare, and he even makes room for true individuals: *sui generis* types that are never instantiated again.

Throughout his writings, Nietzsche commends what he calls "an enchanting abundance of types, a lavish profusion of forms in change and at play" (TI "Anti-nature" 6). There are higher and lower men. There are slaves, nobles, and priests. Philosophers are often discussed as a type, as are free spirits, free thinkers, and good Europeans. There is the overman, and his blinking counterpart, the last man. Nietzsche also discusses poets as a type, as well as saints and nihilists. The fourth book of *Thus Spoke Zarathustra* is a veritable menagerie of types: the king, the leech, the magician, the retired pope, the ugliest human, the voluntary beggar, and the shadow. Finally, there are the eponymous types: the Apollonian, Dionysian, Socratic, Christian, and Kantian, along with the Schopenhauers, Buddhas, Napoleons, Cesare Borgias, and Goethes. For Nietzsche, the fact of human diversity is worthy of celebration, and part of what it means to cultivate virtue is to sharpen and crystalize what is distinctive of one's type – and not to strive in vain for virtues that are appropriate to another's type.

At the same time, Nietzsche deplores the impulse, which he associates with moralizing, to deny the enchanting abundance of types. According to TI "Anti-nature" 6, the moralist responds to the abundance of types by shouting, "no! people should be *different from the way they are*." The moralist "even knows what people should be like, this miserable fool, he paints a picture of himself on the wall and says 'ecce homo!'" The "immoralist," with whom Nietzsche identifies, is instead open "to all types of understanding, comprehension, *approval.*" In this passage and others, Nietzsche can come across as a critic of virtue. The aim of this Element is to convince you that he is not. Nietzsche criticizes many dispositions that pass for virtues (Creasy 2020, pp. 47–48). He criticizes the homogenization that often accompanies moralizing. But he also celebrates virtues that are fitting to their bearers' types, and he opposes kneejerk reactions to idiosyncratic virtues that so easily lead us to condemn rather than cultivate what is distinctive in ourselves and the people we love. Far from being a critic of virtue, Nietzsche follows in the venerable philosophical tradition of criticizing false virtue and attempting to open up a space for authentic agency. What is most distinctive about his approach is his insistence that universal human nature is a myth, and that therefore we need to relativize our conception of virtue to the type of person who embodies it. Paradoxically, for Nietzsche, universal flourishing is only possible once we give up on a universal pantheon of virtues.

This point is perhaps best made by considering Nietzsche's use of the metaphor of Procrustes' bed. In Greek myth, Procrustes is an obsessive bandit. He invites guests to sleep in his bed, but it is never the right size for them. Instead of acknowledging the fact of human diversity and accommodating his guests, he does violence to them: either stretching them if they are too short for the bed or amputating their legs if they are too tall. Procrustes thus imposes his own norm on everyone in a way that annihilates their capacity to flourish. For Nietzsche, universal moral norms are likewise a Procrustean bed. Moralists, rather than acknowledging the fact of human diversity and accommodating people's dispositions, do violence to them: Forcing or attempting to force them to act in ways contrary to their nature and to feel intense self-condemnatory emotions such as guilt and shame when they do not meet expectations. In *Daybreak* 499, Nietzsche first uses this metaphor:

> 'Only the solitary man is evil!' [...]in the midst of society and sociability every evil inclination has to place itself under such great restraint, don so many masks, lay itself so often on the Procrustean bed of virtue, that one could well speak of a martyrdom of the evil man. In solitude all this falls away. He who is evil is at his most evil in solitude: which is where he is also at his best.

As I explain later, solitude is a distinctively Nietzschean virtue that disposes its bearer to escape from and criticize the norms of their society and culture, especially their un-elective in-groups. It thus makes possible the rejection of Procrustean norms. Nietzsche returns to the figure of Procrustes in *Twilight of the Idols*, "Skirmishes" 43: "A *regressive development* or turnaround in any way, shape, or form is absolutely impossible. This is something that we physiologists, at least, do know. But all priests and moralists have believed that it was possible, – they *wanted* to set humanity back – *to cut humanity down* – to an *earlier* level of virtue. Morality was always a Procrustean bed."

In this passage, Nietzsche goes on to say that progress, which he embraces, demands a descent into "*decadence*," a phenomenon that he consistently associates with individualism and difference.

In the remainder of this introduction, I describe the methodology underlying my approach, then outline the substantive sections of the Element.

Methodology

In recent work, I have pointed out methodological shortcomings in earlier Nietzsche scholarship. I will not rehearse these complaints at length here. The main problem is that many scholars have laid too much emphasis on some concepts and phenomena that Nietzsche has little to say about (e.g., the sovereign individual, resentment, and will to power) while neglecting concepts and phenomena that he discusses at length and in illuminating ways (e.g., curiosity, intellectual courage, having a sense of humor, solitude, and shame). I have recommended using methods from the digital humanities to help correct these gluts and gaps, which has led Miyasaki (2022) to sneer at my "bean-counting" methodology without offering a systematic methodology of his own. Digital humanities experts (Pichler & Reiter 2022) and Nietzsche scholars have been more enthusiastic (Bamford 2020; Cristy 2020; Reginster 2020). As this is an Element about Nietzsche on virtue, I here deploy these methods to contextualize and shed light on what he has to say specifically about virtue. The main idea behind this approach is to get a sense of *which books address virtue, where in any given book virtue is addressed,* and *what else is addressed when virtue is addressed.*

Let's get started by asking where Nietzsche talks about virtue over the course of his philosophical career (Figure 1).

Figure 1 represents the prevalence of the word stem *tugend**, which translates as "virtue." Each of his books is represented as a bubble, where the x-axis shows the year of (final) publication (some books, such as *Human, All-Too-Human*, and *The Gay Science*, were issued multiple times) or authorization and the y-axis shows the percentage of the book that refers to virtue.[1] For instance, just over 0.1 percent of the words in *Twilight of the Idols* begin with *tugend**. Thus,

---

[1] An anonymous reviewer asked whether it is possible to use a double wildcard, searching for *tugend*. Unfortunately, the quanteda package in R that I used to conduct this analysis only allows for wildcards at the end of word stems. This means that handful of words with a prefix before *tugend** are not included. Fortunately, there are only three passages across the entire Nietzsche corpus where such a prefixed word occurs and the unprefixed word does not occur (D

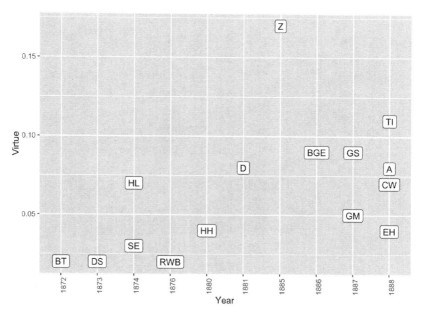

Figure 1 Prevalence of "virtue" [*tugend**] in Nietzsche's writings, as a percentage of the total number of words per book.

we can see that Nietzsche barely addressed virtue in *The Birth of Tragedy* or *David Strauss, The Confessor and the Writer*. He started to become more interested in *The Uses and Disadvantages of History for Life*, resumed that interest in *Daybreak*, and then continued to express interest throughout the remainder of his philosophical career. This is why I will be concentrating on the middle, mature, and late works in this Element.

Figure 2 shows in more detail where Nietzsche talks about virtue in each of these books.

As Figure 2 shows, Nietzsche's writings are littered with talk of virtue. There are also interesting clusters of virtue-talk in various works. For instance, talk of virtue occurs primarily in the first two books of *Thus Spoke Zarathustra*. By contrast, talk of virtue in *Beyond Good and Evil* is concentrated in the second half of the book. *The Antichrist* kicks off with a dense discussion of virtue, while *Twilight of the Idols* addresses virtue more evenly throughout.

Finally, consider Figure 3, which represents the frequency with which Nietzsche addresses fifty other concepts, operationalized via the German word stems he uses to express them, in the same paragraph that he talks about virtue.

392, D 556, GM III:22). Having reviewed these passages again, my interpretation has not changed.

Lexical dispersion plot

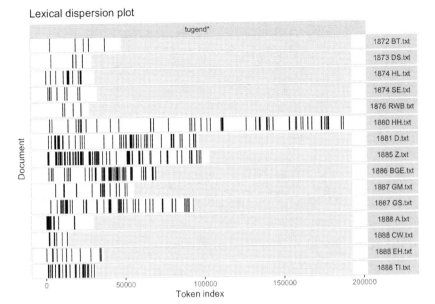

Figure 2 Lexical dispersion of *tugend** in Nietzsche's corpus. Books are represented in chronological order by year of final publication or authorization. The x-axis represents where in each book the word occurs. Since HH is much longer than Nietzsche's other books, its bar is the widest (approximately 200,000 words, in contrast with *Zarathustra*, which is a little over 100,000 words).

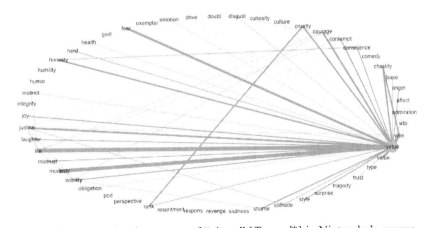

Figure 3 Paragraph-wise egonet of "virtue" [*Tugend**] in Nietzsche's corpus. Edge width = frequency of co-occurrence. Node size = sum of co-occurrences. Abbreviations: "pod" refers to pathos of distance, "respons" refers to responsibility, "wtp" refers to will to power. Terms are arranged alphabetically counter-clockwise.

As Figure 3 shows, when Nietzsche talks about virtue, he also talks about a range of other concepts and phenomena, including chastity, contempt, courage, cruelty, fear, honesty, justice, life, modesty, nobility, rank, shame, solitude, value, and vice. Of course, the mere fact that he talks about these concepts in the same paragraph doesn't tell us how he thinks they are related. But it does tell us that any adequate interpretation of Nietzsche on virtue ought to have something to say about these concepts.

Outline

In the next section, I articulate Nietzsche's understanding of human types. I argue that, for Nietzsche, a type is a constellation of instincts and other drives. Different people embody different types because they have different sets of drives or drives with different strengths. Over the course of Nietzsche's philosophical career, he grew more and more interested in instincts, which he seems to think are not susceptible to significant modification through enculturation or individual learning and effort. This insight leads to the next section, which spells out Nietzsche's type-relative virtue theory. If virtue is the health of the soul, and different souls belong to different types, then different clusters of dispositions will constitute and count as virtues for different types of people (GS 120). By contrast, denial of type-relativity is associated with Procrustean moralism. Such denial, because it runs contrary to drives and instincts that are difficult or even impossible to change, is life-denying. It tells people to be a way that they cannot be, and can easily lead to visceral self-condemnation in the form of guilt and shame. In the next section, I show how enmeshed the development and evaluation of our drives is with our social relationships. In particular, I argue that, for Nietzsche, virtues are constructed in at least two ways. First, sometimes we self-attribute virtues that we don't (quite) possess, then receive social affirmation, which leads us to fully embody the traits in question. Second, sometimes others attribute virtues to us that we don't (quite) possess, then receive uptake from us, which again leads us to fully embody the traits in question. In other words, sometimes virtue attributions – both self-attributions and attributions to others – function as self-fulfilling prophecies. Thus, despite being an individualist, Nietzsche held that the conditions for the possibility of developing and possessing virtue are social. In the final section, I argue that, in order to flourish, one needs to understand one's own type, so that one can pursue a life consistent with one's type. But there are shameful aspects of all of us, so it takes a kind of cruel curiosity and intellectual courage – not to mention a sense of humor to lighten the mood – to gain the self-knowledge required for flourishing. In addition, taking others seriously as individuals in our relationships with them, and understanding the cultural norms that lead people to attempt to live in ways inconsistent with their types, requires curiosity about others, their ways of life, and alternative norms they might adopt. This in turn leads to Nietzsche's attempts at cultural criticism through solitude. Nietzsche desperately wants to help at least some contemporaries and future generations to stop despising aspects of themselves that cannot be changed, to embrace *amor fati*, or love of fate (GS 276, EH "Clever" 10, EH "Books" CW 4). Thus, he combines intense individualism in his embrace of diverse types with a no-less-intense concern for the well-being of others. Indeed, far from being an egoist, Nietzsche was deeply troubled by the stymying of human capability and flourishing that flows from Procrustean moralism.

2 Drives, Instincts, and Types

In this section, I articulate Nietzsche's conceptions of drives, instincts, and types.

Drives

For Nietzsche, drives motivate the agents who embody them to act by influencing their affective orientations (Reginster 2006; Katsafanas 2011b, 2013; Alfano 2019). A Nietzschean drive has both an aim and – in moments of expression – an object. In this framework, drives are individuated by their aims or distinctive forms of activity. A drive disposes one to activate behavior of a particular type, though not necessarily with respect to any particular intentional object. Affects, which orient us to the evaluative character of our situation, trigger, and shape the occurrent expression of a drive. As Katsafanas (2016) says, "The drive itself is indifferent to the object; the drive simply seeks expression. So the aggressive drive will seek to vent itself on whatever object happens to be present." A drive, according to Janaway, is a "relatively stable tendency to activate behavior of some kind" (2007, p. 214), but the object on which that behavior is activated is left unspecified. Janaway (2007, p. 158) also argues that drives are individuated by the range of actions associated with their objects.

Hunger, thirst, the drive to form social bonds, and the sex drive are among the strongest and most universal. Their biological basis is also very deep, though even these drives are to some extent influenced by enculturation and can be indirectly (and sometimes even directly) steered by the individual. Other, less biologically basic drives, such as the drive to dominate, inquisitiveness, and the drive to conform (what Nietzsche calls the herd instinct), are extremely common if not universal. And they too can be shaped to a somewhat greater extent by enculturation and by individual learning and effort. All of these drives are shared with nonhuman animals of various species, especially other mammals.

Drives are individuated by their characteristic aims. The sex drive and the drive to dominate, for instance, differ in their generic aims. In addition, a drive with some distinctive aim sometimes finds expression on a particular object. Thus, drives don't aim at a single predetermined state of affairs. Instead, they aim at more general states of affairs, many of which involve the exercise of one's own agency.[2] And as Nietzsche points out in D 119, some drives are less and others more promiscuous in their selection of objects. Hunger, at one end of the spectrum, is "in earnest" in not being "content with *dream food*." By contrast, other drives can be contented, at least for a time, by dreams and fantasies.

Evidence for this understanding of drives crops up in multiple passages. Arguably the most detailed passage about drives in all of Nietzsche's writings is D 109, which catalogs six ways to modulate or steer a drive:

> First, one can avoid opportunities for gratification of the drive, and through long and ever longer periods of non-gratification weaken it and make it wither away. Then, second, one can impose upon oneself strict regularity in its gratification: by thus imposing a rule upon the drive itself and enclosing its ebb and flood within firm time-boundaries, one has then gained intervals during which one is no longer troubled by it [. . . .] Third, one can deliberately give oneself over to the wild and unrestrained gratification of a drive in order to generate disgust with it and with disgust to acquire a power over the drive. [. . .] Fourth, there is the intellectual artifice of associating its gratification in general so firmly with some very painful thought that, after a little practice, the thought of its gratification is itself at once felt as very painful [. . .] Fifth, one brings about a dislocation of one's quanta of strength by imposing on oneself a particularly difficult and strenuous labor, or by deliberately subject-ing oneself to a new stimulus and pleasure and thus directing one's thoughts and plays of physical forces into other channels. [. . .] Finally, sixth: he who can endure it and finds it reasonable to weaken and depress his *entire* bodily and physical organization will naturally thereby also attain the goal of weakening an individual violent drive.

In this passage, Nietzsche explores ways to manage one's drives. He is preoccu-pied with the same question in BGE 189, where he claims that temporarily starving a drive purifies and sharpens it. What do these metaphors of starving, purifying, and sharpening amount to? Starving refers to blocking or forbidding the most natural way of expressing the drive (the first of the six methods in D 109), whereas purification and sharpening refer to the ways in which the drive

---

[2] Thanks to an anonymous reviewer for helping me to clarify this point.

nevertheless finds expression in some other, less easily recognized or easily accomplished way (the second of the six methods in D 109). According to Nietzsche, this explains the paradox of "why it was precisely during the most Christian period of Europe and altogether under the pressure of Christian value judgments that the sex drive sublimated itself into love (*amour-passion*)." Forbidden expression through carnal intercourse, the sex drive did not disappear or dissipate, but instead found a new way to express itself.

In both *Beyond Good and Evil* and the *Genealogy of Morals*, Nietzsche makes a similar argument about aggressive drives. He claims that these drives do not disappear during the political shift into the "straitjacket" of strict social norms; instead, the drives remain but end up expressing themselves differently (GM II:2). "After the structure of society is fixed on the whole and seems secure against external dangers," he claims, "strong and dangerous drives, like an enterprising spirit, foolhardiness, vengefulness, craftiness, rapacity, and the lust to rule, which had so far not merely been honored insofar as they were socially useful [. . .] but had to be trained and cultivated [. . .] are now experienced as dangers" (BGE 201). Indeed, they are "doubly dangerous, since the channels to divert them are lacking." The supposition here is that aggressive drives, lacking an opportunity for discharge in action against an external enemy, will be "diverted" from their usual "channels" onto members of the society or onto oneself. Nietzsche makes a similar claim about aggressive drives in GM II:16: with the establishment of a strictly regulated society, he says, people's

> instincts were disvalued and 'suspended.' [. . .] they no longer possessed their former guides, their regulating, unconscious and infallible drives: [. . .] at the same time the old instincts had not suddenly ceased to make their usual demands! Only it was hardly or rarely possible to humor them: as a rule they had to seek new and, as it were, subterranean gratifications.

Nietzsche's insight is that we embody drives that sometimes lead us to act in ways that undermine our well-being. When aggressive drives turn inward, they can lead to self-harm and emotional distress like guilt.

Nietzsche is aware that such actions can be disastrous and criticized as unreasonable (GS 21, TI "Socrates" 8–9). Why not, when faced with such unreasonableness, just modify one's own drives? At first blush, it might seem that someone with a catastrophe-prone drive could just redirect it (modifying its aim), downregulate it (making it require fewer or less extreme expressions), or expunge it (eliminating it altogether). People are often able to modify their desires and preferences in light of information and feedback. If the bread you're about to eat turns out to be moldy, your desire to eat it quickly dissipates. Why aren't drives responsive to information and feedback in the same way?

Nietzsche thinks that drives are unresponsive or less responsive to information and feedback because of the way in which they and the affects and emotions through which they vent themselves are embodied. He distinguishes between the embodied "quantum of dammed-up energy waiting to be used up somehow" and "something quite insignificant, mostly a small accident in accordance with which this quantum 'discharges' itself in one particular way" (GS 360). The bodily excitations associated with drives and affects constitute chemical and biological modifications that run their course more or less ballistically once triggered. Embodied preparations for action such as increased heart rate, more variable heart rate, skin conductance, vagal tone, risk-aversion versus risk-seeking orientation, approach versus avoidance orientation, and so on are generally not subject to direct, top-down, and voluntary control.

Two aphorisms from *Beyond Good and Evil* drive this point home. The first is BGE 76: "Under peaceful conditions a warlike man sets upon himself." What makes someone warlike is the possession of aggressive drives. A warlike man sets upon himself in peaceful conditions because his aggressive drive does not disappear when its intentional object (the enemy) is unavailable. Instead, the sensations and affects remain, prompting him to find a new object: himself. The other relevant aphorism is BGE 159: "One *has* to repay good and ill – but why precisely to the one who has done us good or ill?" This enigmatic nugget is best understood in terms of drive-displacement. One begins with an urge to repay another person with good (ill), but one is unable to express that urge. The object is unavailable or otherwise prohibited, but the embodied vengeful (grateful) psychological state remains and is displaced onto someone or something else.

Types

If drives are dispositions to act and evaluate, and if a given agent embodies some drives but not others, then we can understand an agent's type as the set of drives they embody in much the same way that in contemporary personality psychology a trait is an interrelated structure of more basic psychological dispositions (thoughts, feelings, emotions, and action-tendencies). On this understanding of types, a type is an interrelated structure of more basic psychological dispositions (instincts and other drives). Building on Nietzsche's frequent association of a person's drives with their type, Leiter (2002) argues that Nietzsche is committed to a "doctrine of types," according to which "each person has a fixed psycho-physical constitution, which defines him as a particular *type* of person." He further argues that someone's constitution is a combination of "*physiological* facts about the person" and "facts about the person's unconscious drives or affects."

Let's now turn to Nietzsche's understanding of types. One passage from *Daybreak* is especially instructive: "However far a man may go in self-knowledge, nothing however can be more incomplete than his image of the totality of drives which constitute his being" (D 119).

Your type is the "totality of drives" that "constitutes" your "being." Your type is not dependent on your beliefs, your knowledge, your memories, your culture, or any of a variety of other candidates, though it can be influenced by these to the extent that they affect your drives. What makes you what you are is the constellation of your drives.

Next, a type is a group of humans united by their shared set of distinctive instincts and other drives. The same type will express itself differently in different social, cultural, and political circumstances. Some people exemplify their type in particularly illustrative ways, which makes them worthy of study and perhaps also of emulation or competition. Let's consider some passages that illustrate this idea.

In HH 144, while reflecting on the unflattering portrait he's just painted of the type of the saint, Nietzsche says that it "goes without saying that this depiction of the saint, which is sketched after the average profile of the whole species, can be countered by many depictions which might evoke more pleasant feelings." But, says Nietzsche, exceptions to the rule he's proposing do not express the "pure type," and should therefore be discounted. Then, in HH 214, Nietzsche argues that the ancient Greeks used the type of the bacchante to ennoble their own drives: "Their secret was to honor even sickness as a god if only it had *power*." Later, Nietzsche contrasts "the type of the saint," which he associates with various psychological dispositions, including "a certain narrowness of intellect" (HH 234), with the type of the sage, which he associates with a drive to "supreme intellect" (HH 235). Further on, Nietzsche argues that exemplars of the philo-sophical type, such as Socrates and Plato, are driven to achieve mastery over themselves. Next, in HH AOM 220, Nietzsche again praises the ancient Greeks, this time for their approach to politics, saying that they "demonstrated that wonderful sense for the factual and typical that later qualified them to become natural scientists, historians, geographers and philosophers." What did this sense allow them to see? It showed them "the natural drives that find expression in their evil qualities," i.e., "all their passions and evil natural inclinations," which they regarded as "all-too-human" and "inescapable," and thus as something to be steered and managed, not quashed entirely. Finally, in HH "Pref" 3, Nietzsche claims that a successful exemplar of "the type 'free spirit' […] has had its decisive experience in a *great liberation* and that previously it was all the more a fettered spirit and seemed to be chained for ever to its pillar and corner." What are such exemplars liberated from? Their longstanding affects, emotions, and passions: "that reverence proper to youth, that reserve and delicacy before all that is honored and revered from of old, that gratitude for the soil out of which they have grown, for the hand which led them, for the holy place where they learned to worship." Moreover, in the moment of liberation, "A drive and impulse rules and masters [the youthful soul] like a command; a will and desire awakens to go off, anywhere, at any cost; a vehement dangerous curiosity for the undiscovered world flames and flickers in its senses." In this semiautobiographical passage, Nietzsche identifies a type (the free spirit) with its characteristic affects, emotions, passions, and instincts and other drives. Consider the psychology Nietzsche attributes to the free spirit in the moment of liberation:

> A sudden terror and suspicion of what it loved, a lightning-bolt of contempt for what is called 'duty', a rebellious, arbitrary, volcanically erupting desire for travel, strange places, estrangements, coldness, soberness, frost, a hatred of love, perhaps a desecrating blow and glance *backwards* to where it formerly loved and worshiped [. . . . He is] full of curiosity and the desire to tempt and experiment [. . . .] Solitude encircles and embraces him, ever more threatening, suffocating, heart-tightening.

Like many of Nietzsche's prefaces, this passage illuminates several drives that constitute virtues in Nietzsche's own type: curiosity, courage, pathos of distance, a contemptuous sense of humor, and solitude.

Moving on from *Human, All-Too-Human*, there are several passages in *Daybreak* that further illuminate what a Nietzschean type is and how types relate to instincts and other drives. First, in D 168 Nietzsche says that he prefers Thucydides to Plato because Thucydides "takes the most comprehensive and impartial delight in all that is typical in men and events and believes that to each type there pertains a quantum of *good sense*: *this* he seeks to discover." Next, Nietzsche examines a different eponymous type: "As the personification [*Typus*] of a single drive worked through to the end with perfect consistency, Napoleon belongs to the mankind of antiquity: Its characteristic signs – the simple construction and the inventive elaboration and variation of a single motif or of a few motifs – can easily be recognized in him."

Next, In BGE 2, Nietzsche questions the "typical prejudgment" of metaphysicians who reject the possibility that anything could arise out of its opposite, and who therefore make characteristic (false) judgments, saying that "this kind of valuation looms in the background of all their logical procedures; it is on account of this 'faith' that they trouble themselves about 'knowledge', about something that is finally baptized solemnly as 'the truth'." Later, in BGE 26, Nietzsche suggests that someone who both belongs to a higher type and seeks knowledge may at first be reluctant to study lower types, but that such a person will eventually say to himself, "the rule is more interesting than the exception – than myself, the exception!" In BGE 37, Nietzsche diagnoses the religious type as the sort of person who seems to switch violently from vice to virtue: An exemplar of this type is merely, he argues, expressing the same drive in different ways or under different modes of social evaluation. And in BGE 62, Nietzsche argues that "the higher the type of man that a man represents, the greater the improbability that he will turn out *well*."

He then goes on to complain that the Christian approach to suffering lacks what he elsewhere calls the pathos of distance ("not noble enough to see the abysmally different order of rank, chasm of rank, between man and man"), and has therefore bred "a smaller, almost ridiculous type [*Art*], a herd animal." In other words, Christianity encourages Procrustean moralism insofar as it does not recognize that different ways of life are conducive to the flourishing of different types of people, actively seeking the homogenization of humanity.

In BGE 105, Nietzsche characterizes the free spirit as a type distinguished by its disposition to experience particular judgments and emotions. In BGE 186, he advocates the detailed construction of a "*typology* of morals" that would "order the tremendous realm of tender value feelings and value distinctions that live, grow, reproduce, and are destroyed." In BGE 200, Nietzsche discusses the eponymous type he associates with Caesar. Next, in BGE 257, Nietzsche argues that "Every enhancement of the type 'man' has so far been the work of an aristocratic society [. . .] that believes in the long ladder of an order of rank and differences in value between man and man, and that needs slavery in some sense or other." In other words, a society that accepts that there are different types of people for whom different ways of life are conducive to flourishing. According to BGE 260, this pathos of distance enforces the distinction between nobility and contemptibility. Someone who embodies this pathos, such as the hero of a Viking saga, belongs to "a type of man [that] is *not* made for pity, and the hero of the saga therefore adds as a warning: 'If the heart is not hard in youth it will never harden.'" Nietzsche goes on to say that the exemplar of this type is driven by the "necessity for having enemies (as it were, as drainage ditches for the affects of envy, quarrelsomeness, exuberance – at bottom, in order to be capable of being good *friends*): all these are typical characteristics of noble morality." Here we see once again that Nietzsche associates a type with the instincts, drives, and affects that distinguish it, and that these psychological states are bound to express themselves on one object (the "drainage ditch") if they cannot express themselves on another.

A couple of passages later, Nietzsche again speaks of types and the dispositions that constitute them in biological terms:

> A *kind* [*Art*] comes to be, a type [*Typus*] becomes fixed and strong, through the long fight with essentially constant *unfavorable* conditions. Conversely, we know from the experience of breeders that species accorded superabundant nourishment and quite generally extra protection and care soon tend most strongly towards variations of the type and become rich in marvels and monstrosities (including monstrous vices). Now look for once at an aristocratic commonwealth – say, an ancient Greek *polis*, or Venice – as an arrangement, whether voluntary or involuntary, for *breeding*: human beings are together there who are dependent on themselves and want their kind to prevail, most often because they *have to* prevail or run the terrible risk of being exterminated. Here that boon, that excess, and that protection which favor variations are lacking; the kind needs itself as a kind, as something that can prevail and make itself durable by virtue of its very hardness, uniformity, and simplicity of form, in a constant fight with its neighbors or with the oppressed who are rebellious or threaten rebellion. Manifold experience teaches them to which qualities above all they owe the fact that, despite all gods and men, they are still there, that they have always triumphed: these qualities they call virtues, these virtues alone they cultivate. (BGE 262)[italic in the original]

Nietzsche here characterizes types with the language of heredity, associating a type with the instincts and other drives that characterize it. Finally, consider BGE 264, in which Nietzsche associates the "plebeian" type with the drives, affects, and emotions common to it: "disgusting incontinence," "nook envy," and "clumsy insistence that one is always right."

We now move on to the *Genealogy*. In GM I:5, Nietzsche says that people who belong to the noble type sometimes designate themselves by a *"typical character trait,"* such as their power, wealth, or honesty. In GM III:7, Nietzsche suggests that Schopenhauer was typical of philosophers in his instinctive hatred of sensuality. He says that every animal "instinctively strives for an optimum of favorable conditions under which it can expend all its strength and achieve its maximal feeling of power; every animal abhors, just as instinctively and with a subtlety of discernment that is 'higher than all reason,' every kind of intrusion or hindrance that obstructs or could obstruct this path to the optimum."

Once again, Nietzsche defines a type by its distinctive instincts, which he associates with biological properties of the type. In GM III:10, he addresses the "contemplative type" of man, of which philosophers are a subtype: "The inactive, brooding, unwarlike element in the instincts of contemplative men long surrounded them with a profound mistrustfulness: the only way of dispelling it was to arouse a decided *fear* of oneself." And in GM III:11, Nietzsche identifies the priestly type with a defining "instinct": commitment to the ascetic ideal. A couple of passages later, he returns to this point, saying that "*the ascetic ideal springs from the protective instinct of a degenerating life* that tries by all means to sustain itself and to fight for its existence; it indicates a partial physiological obstruction and exhaustion against which the deepest instincts of life [...] continually struggle" (GM III:13).

In *The Antichrist*, Nietzsche says that "Epicurus is a *typical* decadent [....] The fear of pain, even of infinitesimal amounts of point – this could end up *only* as a *religion of love*," which means that Epicurus is the Greek equivalent of Christ, who embodied the "*instinct of hatred for reality*" and the "*instinctive exclusion of all aversion, all hostility, all boundaries and distances in feeling*" (A 30). Nietzsche here diagnoses these instincts as consequences of "extreme over-sensitivity and capacity for suffering." Types crop up in many other passages of this Element. In A 3, for example, Nietzsche asks "what type of human being should be *bred*" and suggests that "out of terror" at this more valuable type, "the opposite type was willed, bred, *achieved*: the domestic animal, the herd animal, the sick animal: man, – the Christian." Later, he indicts Christianity because it "has waged a *war to the death* against this *higher* type of person, it has banned all the basic instincts of this type, it has distilled 'evil' and 'the Evil One' out of these instincts" (A 5). In this way, Christianity "has made an ideal out of whatever *contradicts* the preservation instincts of a strong life; it has corrupted the reason of even the most spiritual natures by teaching people to see the highest spiritual values as sinful." Various other types also crop up in this Element. In A 12, Nietzsche says that "the philosopher is just a further development of the priestly type. In A 29, Nietzsche calls Jesus the "type of the redeemer," in whom the "polar opposite of struggle, of any feeling of doing-battle, has become instinct." Finally, in A 54, Nietzsche condemns the faithful type of person for its characteristic epistemic instincts and drives.

Turn now to *Twilight of the Idols*. In TI "Socrates" 2, Nietzsche indicts Socrates and Plato, saying that "the great sages are *types of decline*." In TI "Anti-nature" 6, he condemns those who, following Procrustean moralism, would reduce the variety of human types to a single way of living and flourishing: Let us think how naïve it is to say 'this is the way people *should* be!'. Reality shows us an enchanting abundance of types, a lavish profusion of forms in change and at play: and some worthless idiot of a moralist sees all this and says: 'no! people should be *different from the way they are*!?'"

While Nietzsche clearly thinks there are type-based constraints on how someone can live and act, he also recognizes that types are "in change and at play." It is not a trivial matter to regiment this abundance of types: People differ from each other in significant ways, and the difficulty (though not the impossibility) of some sort of Procrustean social, political, or moral policy would do violence to a great many individuals. Finally, Nietzsche suggests that the very fact of the *diversity* of types is itself valuable.

In "Skirmishes of an Untimely Man," Nietzsche engages with a variety of types. He calls Thomas Carlyle a "typical romantic" (TI "Skirmishes" 12). He diagnoses aesthetic hatred and disgust with "exhaustion, heaviness, age, fatigue, every time freedom is lacking, as with cramps, paralysis, and above all the smell, the color, the form of disintegration, of putrefaction" in one's own type as the "deepest instinct" of that type. And he diagnoses the "criminal type" as "a strong type of person under unfavorable conditions, a strong person made ill. [. . .] His *virtues* are ostracized by society; his liveliest drives quickly fuse with depressive affects, with suspicion, fear, dishonor."

Finally, let's turn to *Ecce Homo*. In EH "Clever" 3, Nietzsche identifies the skeptics as a type in ancient Greece. In the next passage, he argues that Shakespeare conceived the type of Caesar because he was able to empathize with Caesar's drives and affects. In EH "Clever" 5, Nietzsche accuses Wagner of representing the type of the decadent. In EH "Books" 1, Nietzsche says that the overman is a type that has the "highest constitutional excellence, in contrast to 'modern' people, to 'good' people, to Christians and other nihilists." In EH "Books" BT 1, he associates Socrates with the "typical decadent" for pitting "'rationality' *against* instinct." He says that Zarathustra represents a type (EH "Books" Z 1), and that this type embodies *"great health"* which expresses itself as several virtues (courage, cheerfulness, and curiosity) and characteristic emotions (malice, high spirits, and the feeling that "everything that was considered great about people lies infinitely far *beneath* him"). In "Books" BGE.2, Nietzsche describes *Beyond Good and Evil* as a *"critique of modernity"* and an indication of Zarathustra, "an opposite type who is as un-modern as possible, a noble, affirmative type." In EH "Destiny" 4, Nietzsche argues that the condition for the possibility of the last man, another type, is "the *lie*: – to put it another way, taking all measures to *avoid* seeing that reality is *not* constituted in a way that always invites benevolent instincts." He then contrasts the last man with the type of Zarathustra and the overman, whom he calls "the type that conceives of reality *as it is*: his type has the strength to do this" (EH "Destiny" 5).

3 Type-Relative Virtue Theory

The notion that Nietzsche is a virtue theorist was first popularized in Anglophone philosophy by Walter Kaufmann (1968). Kaufmann claims that "Nietzsche's debt to Aristotle's ethics" – especially to the Aristotelian conception of *megalopsy-chia,* which foreshadows Nietzsche's overman – is "considerable" (p. 384).

Although Bernd Magnus (1980) dismantled the superficial connection between the great-souled man and the overman, many commentators still think it's plausible to construe Nietzsche as a virtue theorist of some stripe or other.[3] We shall see that he's best understood as deploring many of the traditional virtues while admiring "virtue in the style of the Renaissance, *virtù*, moraline-free virtue" (A 2). However, most discussions of Nietzsche as a virtue theorist have addressed him only piecemeal, and some of the direct engagements with Nietzsche and the construct of *virtue* have unfortunately tended to stray quite far from the text or to build a whole interpretation on just a few passages (e.g., Swanton 2015).

Expressing our drives is deeply tied to our capacity to live and flourish, though that does not mean that every expression is conducive to well-being. Without hunger, we would perish, but in our modern nutrient-rich environment, hunger can also lead to obesity and diabetes. Without thirst, we would die, but people under the effects of MDMA sometimes feel intense and unnecessary thirst that leads to overhydration. For Nietzsche, a drive or interrelated structure of drives constitutes a virtue in certain circumstances.

Various commentators have discussed the dispositions needed to live well in Nietzsche's philosophy by focusing on drives and their interrelations. This work tends to articulate normative ideals via the constructs of life, health, or integrity. For example, Andrew Huddleston (2017) argues that, for Nietzsche, the ideal of spiritual health is a matter of having strong and unified drives that point the agent in the direction of worthwhile activity. John Richardson (1996) argues that Nietzsche prizes the integration of drives into a unity that is fundamentally active. Ken Gemes (2009) argues that Nietzsche's ideal is the imposition of order on one's psychic economy by a "master drive," which harnesses and controls the expression of other drives rather than suppressing them. According to Gemes (2013, p. 568), "The healthiest (highest) life involves the maximal expression of the richest set of drives." Lanier Anderson argues that, "Nietzschean strength *in general* is a matter of the integration of the self's drives and desires so that they cohere to form a genuine self, or individual." Katsafanas (2011a) also argues that Nietzsche prizes integration, but on his interpretation what gets integrated is not the agent's drives (with one another) but her drives and conscious thoughts. In particular, integration obtains when the agent's attitude toward her own drive-motivated actions is stable under the revelation of further information about the action's etiology. For instance, consider someone who excels at artistic production, which is (unbeknownst to her) motivated by a drive to do or appear better than others on some valued dimension (as in D 30). Then ask whether she would continue to value her

---

[3] See Hurka (2007), May (1999), Reginster (2015), and White (2001), among others.

artistic production if she were to become aware of why she engaged in it. According to Katsafanas, if such knowledge would undermine her positive evaluation of her own actions, then she is not integrated; if, however, such knowledge would leave her evaluative stance intact, she is integrated.

In this section, I develop and articulate a version of the integration thesis described earlier. In particular, I argue that a Nietzschean virtue is a well-calibrated instinct or other drive. A drive is well-calibrated when it satisfies two integration conditions. First, a drive enjoys *agentic integration* to the extent that its expression is consistent with the expression of the agent's other drives. Call this *weak agentic integration*. In cases of *strong agentic integration*, the expression of one of the agent's drives is at the same time an expression of one or more of the agent's other drives. An example of strong agentic integration is Nietzsche's combination of curiosity and intellectual courage: When he expresses his inquisitiveness, he often does so in the context of inquiry that reveals truths that are hard to stomach, so by manifesting curiosity he at the same time manifests intellectual courage. For a more mundane example, consider someone who integrates their sex drive with their drive to dominate by taking a dominant role in sexual encounters. Second, a drive contributes to *evaluative integration* to the extent that it does not systematically or reliably induce negative self-directed emotions (e.g., guilt, shame) that respond to fixed aspects of the self (i.e., certain of one's drives). When these negative emotions are absent, the drive enjoys *weak evaluative integration*. When, in addition, the agent also experiences positive self-directed emotions (e.g., pride, self-affirmation) that respond to fixed aspects of the self, we can call that *strong evaluative integration*, which is closely related to what Nietzsche sometimes calls *amor fati*.[4] Someone who enjoys both agentic and evaluative integration thereby satisfies the normative criteria for what Nietzsche frequently calls life or health.[5]

As we will see in the next section, because Nietzsche thinks that our self-understanding is deeply and essentially tied to our relationship with our community, he thinks that evaluative integration is only possible if one's community does not systematically prompt one to experience shame or guilt about one's

---

[4] This interpretation is consistent with and can be seen as a refinement of Hunt's (1993, p. 113) claim that "For Nietzsche, one's virtues belong uniquely to oneself. One discovers which virtues are one's own by discovering the goals toward which one's psychic energies should be directed. [...] virtue is a certain complete integration of the psyche."

[5] I do not have space here to address exactly what Nietzsche means by life and health, as well as their relationship to flourishing and the will to power. That they are tightly interwoven, if not identical, is very clear from Nietzsche's writings. However, he is often frustratingly vague about what he means by life and health. Thanks to an anonymous reviewer for pressing me on this point. For the purposes of this element, I will treat them as interchangeable.

unchangeable characteristics, especially one's instincts and other drives. If someone attempts, perhaps through social pressure, to embody a drive in a way that is incompatible with her type, to act in a way that systematically or reliably induces negative emotions about her own drives, or to express drives in a way that systematically or reliably meets with intense social and moral disapproval (especially disapproval that she is liable to internalize), she will not turn out well.

Since types are constellations of drives, different virtues are fitting for people who belong to different types. Thus, Nietzsche held a *type-relative unity of virtue thesis*, according to which someone's flourishing is a matter of developing and acting from character traits that fit her type. Since people have different types, some will find it easier to embody virtue in one social context while others will find it easier to do so in another context.

In this section, I also argue that Nietzsche was an exemplarist virtue theorist. In his framework, exemplars of different types elicit different emotions in people with fine-tuned affective sensitivity. While some exemplars inspire admiration that leads to emulation, others elicit respect, pride, or what Nietzsche calls the pathos of distance. Still others incite envy and the motivation to agonistic one-upsmanship. Exemplars of bad or deplorable types provoke contempt and disgust, which serve as signposts of what to avoid. Thus, Nietzschean exemplarism offers a richer, more evaluatively and motivationally nuanced moral psychology than the contemporary monochrome admire-and-emulate model.

Nietzsche's Person-Type-Relative Unity of Virtue Thesis

To elucidate these ideas, let's start with HH 99, which suggests that instincts overlap with both drives and virtues: "Morality is preceded by *compulsion* [. . . .] Later it becomes custom, later still voluntary obedience, finally almost instinct: then, like all that has for a long time been habitual and natural, it is associated with pleasure – and is now called *virtue*." According to this passage, a pattern of behavior that is initially coerced, then customary, then voluntary, is eventually internalized to such an extent that it emerges from instinct. Here, we see Nietzsche's first articulation of the idea that a drive accompanied by positive affect is a virtue.

Turning to *Daybreak*, we find Nietzsche arguing in D 26 that, "The beginnings of justice, as of prudence, moderation, bravery – in short, of all we designate as the *Socratic virtues*, are *animal*: a consequence of that drive which teaches us to seek food and elude enemies." Virtues are here consequences of drives. Their instinctual adaptiveness in pursuit of the nutrition and security that foster life and health makes them virtues. Nietzsche goes on to say that "if we consider that even the highest human being has only become more elevated and subtle in the nature of his food and in his conception of what is inimical to him, it is not improper to describe the entire phenomenon of morality as animal." Next, in GS 17, Nietzsche suggests that even weaknesses can virtues if they are calibrated to the rest of the agent's psychological set. Later, in GS 120, Nietzsche revises and relativizes the dictum "virtue is the health of the soul" to "*your* virtue is the health of *your* soul."

Next, in Z I "Chastity," we read "In some people chastity is a virtue, but in many it is almost a vice," and what determines this is the agent's drive set. Nietzsche makes a similar point through the character of Zarathustra at greater length in Z I "Passions of Pleasure and Pain":

> My brother, if you have one virtue, and it is your virtue, then you have it in common with no one.
>
> To be sure, you want to call her by name and caress her; you want to tug at her ear and have fun with her.
>
> And behold! Now you have her name in common with the people and have become the people and the herd with your virtue!
>
> You would do better to say: "Unspeakable and nameless is that which causes my soul agony and sweetness and is even the hunger of my entrails."
>
> Let your virtue be too high for the familiarity of names, and if you must speak of it, then do not be ashamed to stammer about it.
>
> Then speak and stammer: "This is *my* good, I love this, thus I like it entirely, thus alone do I want the good.
>
> I do not want it as a divine law, I do not want it as a human statue and requirement. It shall be no signpost for me to overearths and paradises.
>
> It is an earthly virtue that I love: there is little prudence in it and least of all the reason of the many.
>
> But this bird built its nest in my house, therefore I love and caress it, now it sits next to me on its golden eggs."
>
> Thus you should stammer and praise your virtue.
>
> Once you had passions and named them evil. But now you have only your virtues: they grew out of your passions.
>
> You set your highest goal at the heart of these passions, and then they became your virtues and passions of pleasure.
>
> And whether you stemmed from the clan of the irascible or the lascivious or the fanatic or the vengeful:
>
> Ultimately all your passions became virtues and all your devils became angels.

In this passage, Zarathustra urges his audience to cherish virtues that are fitting to their natures, indeed to their individuality. In other passages, he suggests that some virtues might be suitable for more than one person, but this passage poignantly expresses the idea that in some cases they really may be unique.

Another relevant passage from *Zarathustra* is "On the virtuous," where Zarathustra instructs his followers, "That your virtue is your self and not something foreign, a skin, a cloak, that is the truth from the foundation of your souls, you who are virtuous." Here the character of Zarathustra insists that virtue is relative to its possessor's type, contrary to the universalizing perspective of Procrustean moralism. Hinting at the importance of the virtue of curiosity, which I discuss further in the following, in Z I "On the bestowing virtue" 2, Zarathustra tells his disciples, "all instincts become sacred in the seeker of knowledge; the soul of the elevated one becomes gay." This passage supports the evaluative integration constraint on virtue.

Different types require different material and social conditions to flourish. Higher types in particular, says Nietzsche, are especially fragile and thus liable to turn out poorly. Moving on to BGE 199, Nietzsche says that the "herd man" glorifies his own herd-instinct and related "attributes, which make him tame, easy to get along with, and useful to the herd, as if they were the truly human virtues: namely, public spirit, benevolence, consideration, industriousness, moderation, modesty, indulgence, and pity." Once again, an instinct is counted as a virtue, at least by and for certain types of people. The hint in this passage, of course, is that other instincts that would suit someone to commanding rather than obeying might also be virtues (for other types of people). Just two sections later, Nietzsche refers to dispositions to "consideration, pity, fairness, mildness, reciprocity" as drives that, starting with Christianity, "receive the honorary designation of 'virtues'." It is clear in this passage that what counts as a virtue simply is a drive that is taken to possess certain special properties by the community of the agent who embodies that drive. Likewise, in BGE 262, Nietzsche argues that communities "call virtues" whatever instincts and other drives have enabled them to survive and triumph.

Next, in BGE 206, Nietzsche asks, "what is the scientific man?" and answers, an ignoble type of person with the virtues that an ignoble type will have: this type is not dominant, authoritative, or self-sufficient. He is industrious, he is patiently lined up in an orderly array, he is regular and moderate in his abilities and needs, he has an instinct for his own kind and for the needs of his kind."

Nietzsche here identifies a type ("the scientific man") and catalogs a set of instincts and other drives that fit the type and therefore are candidate virtues for someone who belongs to that type. In addition, he explicitly refers to the social dimension of evaluative integration: People need social approval or at least not-too-intense disapproval from their community for their drives to count as virtues. Otherwise, they are liable to internalize negative emotions that disqualify their traits from counting as virtues.

In the next passage, Nietzsche says that the "*ideal* scholar in whom the scientific instinct [. . .] blossoms and blooms [. . .] has to pay for these virtues," which include "meeting every thing and experience halfway, the sunny and impartial hospitality with which he accepts everything that comes his way, his type of unscrupulous benevolence, of dangerous unconcern about Yes and No" (BGE 207). Once again, Nietzsche identifies a type (the "ideal scholar") and catalogs a set of instincts and other drives that fit the type and therefore count, when they're expressed and meet with approbation, as virtues for someone of that type.

Next, consider BGE 221. Nietzsche says that "In a person" who embodies the type of the commander, "who is called and made to command, self-denial and modest self-effacement would not be a virtue but the waste of a virtue: thus it seems to me." By contrast, "Every unegoistic morality that takes itself for unconditional and addresses itself to all does not only sin against taste: it is a provocation to sins of omission, one more seduction under the mask of philanthropy – and precisely a seduction and injury for the higher, rarer, privileged." For this reason, he argues, "Moralities must be forced to [admit] that it is immoral to say: 'what is right for one is fair for the other.'" The virtues of someone who belongs to the commanding type are the exact opposite of the virtues of someone whose type involves an ineliminable drive to obedience, which gives the lie to Procrustean moralism. Turning now to the *Genealogy*, consider GM "Pref" 2: "For this alone is fitting for a philosopher. We have no right to isolated acts of any kind: we may not make isolated errors or hit upon isolated truths. Rather do our ideas, our values, our yeas and nays, our ifs and buts, grow out of us with the necessity with which a tree bears fruit."

What's good for someone is to fulfill their type; different people have different types; so what's good for different people is to develop and act from different sets of instincts and other drives. Next, in GM III:7, Nietzsche suggests that Schopenhauer was typical of philosophers in his instinctual hatred of sensuality. In this passage, Nietzsche claims that all animals, including humans, instinctively strive for conditions in which they can express their drives. He also suggests that different types manage to accomplish such activity in different ways that depend on their type. One important way in which someone can fail to fully express their drives is, as he says, through "intrusion or hindrance that obstructs" the expression of the agent's drives. Such a hindrance may be internal (e.g., by expressing one drive, the agent makes it impossible to express another) or external (e.g., expressing the drive leads to death, injury, illness, or social rejection).

In GM III:8, Nietzsche distinguishes between cases in which poverty, humility, and chastity are ersatz and cases in which they are "the most appropriate and natural conditions of [their bearers'] *best* existence, their *fairest* fruitfulness." In the latter cases, the "dominating instinct" of the agent is a kind of "spirituality" which rules over instincts and others drives that express themselves via pride, sensuality, and liberality. The chastity of such people is not motivated by "ascetic scruple or hatred of the senses" but rather by a kind of spiritual "fruitfulness."

Turn now to *The Antichrist* and *Twilight of the Idols*. In the former, Nietzsche asks, "What is happiness?" and answers by saying, "The feeling that power is *growing*, that some resistance is being overcome. *Not* contentedness, but more power; *not* peace, but war; *not* virtue, but proficiency (virtue in the style of the Renaissance, *virtù*, moraline-free virtue)" (A 2). Nietzsche here distinguishes between virtue and *virtù*, and he associates the latter with the expression of the drive he calls "will to power." The implication is that what have been considered virtues in the Christian tradition are somehow counterfeit because they do not adequately express will to power. They undermine agentic and evaluative integration. In A 9, Nietzsche goes on to declare "war" on the "theologian instinct" that, through a "faulty optic" is "made into a morality, a virtue, a holiness." In A 11, Nietzsche again uses derisive scare quotes to distinguish between type-appropriate and type-inappropriate dispositions: "A virtue needs to be our *own* invention, our *own* most personal need and self-defense: in any other sense, a virtue is just dangerous. Whatever is not a condition for life *harms* it." The very same drives that Nietzsche praises as virtues in some people constitute vices in others. If one simply attempts to compile a catalog of all and only the virtues that Nietzsche always praises and never condemns, one comes up empty-handed. However, if one applies a subtler approach, one sees that *within a given type*, his praise is largely consistent.

Finally, in TI "Skirmishes" 37, Nietzsche equates the "loss of any hostile instincts" with "modern 'virtues'," which are "conditioned and *prompted* by weakness." Again, Nietzsche suggests that certain dispositions only count as virtues without really being virtues because they violate the agentic or evaluative integration criteria. In TI "Socrates" 11, Nietzsche claims that, "as long as life is *ascending*, happiness is equal to instinct." Next, consider TI "Errors" 2:

> The most general formula at the center of all religions and moralities is: 'do this, don't do that – and then you'll be happy! Otherwise . . . '. Every morality, every religion, is this imperative, – I call it the great original sin of reason, the immortal unreason. In my mouth, this formula changes into its opposite [. . .] someone who has turned out well, a 'happy one', has to perform certain acts and will instinctively avoid others [. . .] his virtue is the effect of his happiness.

Once again, Nietzsche argues that someone's virtue is a particular way of expressing their instincts. Since different people have different instincts and other drives, the route to flourishing depends on the agent's type. For instance, in TI "Anti-nature" 6, Nietzsche condemns Procrustean moralists who would reduce the variety of human types to a single way of living and flourishing. Individuals flourish by expressing the instincts and other drives distinctive of their types. These passages raise the pessimistic possibility that some types cannot be fulfilled, or at least that it's nearly-impossible to fulfill them. Broken people, whose drives are in such disarray that the expression of one almost inevitably undermines the expression of the others, will find it difficult if not impossible to flourish. "Happy" people, in Nietzsche's view, have all *and only* the virtues they need to express their natures. The more complicated someone's constellation of drives is, the more difficult it will be to express them all.

4 Exemplars in Communities

Nietzsche was an individualist who also cared deeply about how individuals interact with their communities.[6] In this section, I argue that he articulated a distinctive version of exemplarism, which is a theory of how people learn and develop their character by observing and affectively interacting with others. I also argue that the affects that the community directs at the individual shape her character by modulating her instincts and other drives, as well as how she feels about them.

Nietzsche's Polychrome Exemplarism

Exemplarism has a long history in both Christian philosophy and Chinese philosophy. In both traditions, the basic idea is to start not with abstract principles that guide the cultivation and expression of virtue, but with admired individuals, whom one imitates or emulates. In the Christian tradition, the prime exemplar is God. Becoming divine may seem like a tall order, so this version of exemplarism comes with a bridge: the incarnation of Jesus Christ. While emulating the disembodied Father may be intimidating, modeling oneself on the embodied Son is expected to be less daunting. In this model, one begins by admiring the exemplar. Admiration, if it survives reflective scrutiny, motivates the admirer both to understand better the psychic economy of the exemplar and to emulate the exemplar's inner and outer life. Nietzsche's exemplarism is more complex. Admirable exemplars are essentially liminal. On the one hand, they

---

[6] Huddleston (2019) agrees. His book focuses on the virtues *of* communities, that is, of collective agents made up of multiple generations of people who live together and form a culture. He offers few remarks, however, about the virtues of the members of communities.

stake out a field of possibility and potential. On the other hand, they foreclose the prospect of going further. Nietzsche's exemplarism envisions a richer array of both exemplars and emotions directed toward them. In addition, Nietzsche tends to evaluate real and fictionalized exemplars of types, for whom social and cultural context can be supplied – including both those who approximate the ideal of the type (e.g., Caesar, Goethe, and Zarathustra) and those who fail to do so (e.g., Pascal, the wrecks of the higher men in *Zarathustra* book 4).

Consider HL 6. In this passage, Nietzsche refers to the familiar admiration-based notion of exemplarism, saying that "no one has a greater claim to our veneration than he who possesses the drive to and strength for justice. For the highest and rarest virtues are united and concealed in justice as in an unfathomable ocean that receives streams and rivers from all sides and takes them into itself." Later in the same passage, Nietzsche makes clear that by "justice" he has in mind a sort of *epistemic* virtue, which empowers its bearer to make fair and accurate judgments about both axiological matters (what or who is good, bad, virtuous, and vicious) and deontic matters (what must be done). He then asserts that this sort of justice is "the rarest of all virtues," and that it sets its bearer "on a solitary height as the most *venerable* exemplar of the species man; for he desires truth, not as cold ineffectual knowledge, but as a regulating and punishing judge."

Turning now to *Schopenhauer as Educator*, we find two passages of interest: SE 2 and SE 6. In the first, Nietzsche laments the educational system of his time, arguing that it sacrifices the humanity of the youth. As evidence, he points to "the numerous exemplars of those who through an unthinking and premature devotion to science have become crookbacked and humped." He then asks "where are we, scholars and unscholarly, high placed and low, to find the moral exemplars and models for our time?" In this passage, Nietzsche is especially concerned by an over-eager educational system that stuffs its pupils with more knowledge than they can digest and thereby wrecks their psychic economy. Students who, under a different pedagogical regime, might have enjoyed a healthy vitality and become model scholars end up instead crookbacked and humped exemplars. Nietzsche laments their ruination and advocates reforming the educational system in hopes of better cultivating future generations. Thus, in addition to admirable exemplars whom one might emulate, Nietzsche's palette includes pitiable exemplars whose fate one should seek to avoid for oneself and prevent for future generations.

Next, in SE 6, Nietzsche argues that society's "only concern is the individual higher exemplar, the more uncommon, more powerful, more complex, more fruitful." These exemplars are not to be emulated or imitated by just anyone; Nietzsche presupposes that only those who are gifted both in their biological inheritance and in their upbringing and social position have a chance of living up to the standards in play here. For this reason, he suggests that the goal of a species' "evolution lies, not in the mass of its exemplars and their wellbeing, let alone in those exemplars who happen to come last in point of time, but rather in those apparently scattered and chance existences which favorable conditions have here and there produced." If this is right then society "ought to seek out and create the favorable conditions under which those great redemptive men can come into existence."

The next passage in which Nietzsche discusses exemplars is D 549, where he considers several eponymous exemplars. In the context of the Christian (an eponym whose etymology is often forgotten) as well as Shakespeare, Byron, Alexander the Great, Caesar, Mohammed, and Napoleon, Nietzsche here considers a range of "supreme exemplars" of a type of person, where types are, as usual, distinguished and individuated by their characteristic drives (in this case the "impulse to action").

If my interpretation of Nietzsche's emotionally rich exemplarism is on the right track, it also helps to explain Nietzsche's frequent ad hominem attacks. As early as DS, he was lobbing dynamite at his enemies, and he continued to do so throughout his philosophical career. Even the titles of his late works demonstrate this tendency. *The Case of Wagner* (hint: it's not good). *The Antichrist. Nietzsche Contra Wagner.* The "skirmishes" in *Twilight of the Idols*. Nietzsche's predilection for picking on people can make him seem like a petulant, grudge-nursing incel. I don't want to suggest that there is no infusion of personal animus or score-settling in Nietzsche's works, but it's worth reflecting on the fact that, in a letter to his friend Gersdorff, he expressed regret for attacking David Strauss just before he died, saying, "I very much hope that I did not make his last days more difficult and that he died without knowing anything of me." This indicates that Nietzsche sometimes had more sophisticated reasons for attacking individuals.

Just as positive eponymous exemplars showcase the diversity of human types and the ways they can develop and express themselves, so negative eponymous exemplars dramatize either deplorable types or failures to successfully embody a type. In *Twilight of the Idols* "'Improving' Humanity" 2, Nietzsche does just this:

> To call the domestication of an animal an 'improvement' almost sounds like a joke to us. Anyone who knows what goes on in a zoo will have doubts whether beasts are 'improved' there. They become weak, they become less harmful, they are *made ill* through the use of pain, injury, hunger, and the depressive affect of fear. – The same thing happens with domesticated people who have been 'improved' by priests. In the early Middle Ages, when the

church was basically a zoo, the choicest exemplars [*Exemplare*] of the 'blond beast' were hunted down everywhere [. . . .] But what did an 'improved' Teuton look like after being seduced into a cloister? He looked like a caricature of a human being, like a miscarriage: he had turned into a 'sinner', he was stuck in a cage, locked up inside all sorts of horrible ideas . . . . There he lay, sick, miserable, full of malice against himself, hating the drive for life, suspicious of everything that was still strong and happy.

In this passage, Nietzsche uses "the choicest exemplars" to show what happens when someone's drives are turned against themselves. They lack agentic and evaluative integration, which is contrary to their life and health. As we saw earlier, the exemplar is intended not as an object of admiration and emulation but as an object of disgust and contempt.

While reflecting on his own methodology in EH "Wise" 7, Nietzsche explicitly states that this is the point of his ad hominem attacks. In his "practice of war," he says, "I never attack people." This might seem obviously false. The entirety of *David Strauss, the Confessor and the Writer*, is an attack not only on Strauss's book but on Strauss himself. Two of his last books are titled *Nietzsche Contra Wagner* and *The Antichrist*. Yet Nietzsche has a point to make here, even if he gives himself more credit than he likely deserves. To clarify his seemingly outrageous self-characterization, Nietzsche says, "I treat people as if they were high-intensity magnifying glasses that can illuminate a general, though insidious and barely noticeable, predicament." In other words, he treats negative exemplars as highly illustrative case-studies in moral psychology. He goes on: This is how I attacked David Strauss or, more precisely, the *success* of an old and decrepit book in German 'culture', – I caught this culture in the act . . . And this is also how I attacked Wagner or, more precisely, the falseness, the half-couth instincts of our 'culture' that mistakes subtlety for richness and maturity for greatness.

Nietzsche identifies a use of negative exemplars that is both a genuine aspect of his own rhetoric and philosophically interesting and distinctive. His ad hominem attacks make sense when contextualized in his version of exemplarism. When he is at his best, his attacks against individuals aren't really or solely aimed at the individuals themselves. Instead, he targets the types that those individuals exemplify. The individuals serve merely as "high-intensity magnifying glasses that can illuminate a general [. . .] predicament." An individual embodies in lived and socialized reality how a type is liable to develop and express its instincts and other drives.

This suggests several criteria for evaluating the soundness of Nietzsche's ad hominem attacks. First, the individual under attack must genuinely represent the type in question. Second, the flaws diagnosed in the individual must be essential to the type, or at least reliably associated with the ways in which that type is expressed in relevant lived and socialized contexts. Third, the diagnosis must be designed to induce in at least some members of the audience emotions that lead them not to emulate, and indeed in some cases to seek to be and act differently from the negative exemplar. When these conditions are met, an ad hominem attack becomes the use of a negative exemplar. While positive exemplars serve as fingerposts, negative exemplars serve as warning signs.

Virtues in Communities

Several commentators have explored Nietzsche understanding of community and the individual's relation to it. For example, Jessica Berry (2015) explores Nietzsche's admiration for and relationship to his contemporary scientific community through an exemplar of the scientific type: Goethe. Andrew Huddleston (2014) argues that Nietzsche believes that it is in slavish people's own best interest to play a small and distinctly unglorified part in building a communal culture at the top of which are seated exemplars of various higher types. John Richardson (2015) explores the relationship between community and language in Nietzsche's philosophy in illuminating ways. And Avery Snelson (2017) interprets Nietzsche as suggesting that certain moral norms are, or at least have been a condition of community membership, which is why the herd instinct is so prevalent and powerful. Aside from these exceptions, commentators have mostly neglected the importance of community in Nietzsche's moral philosophy.[7] Perhaps this is because Nietzsche is often misperceived as a radical egoist (e.g., by Swanton 2015).

In this section, I argue that one's community and the language used by that community play a constitutive role in the cultivation of virtue. More specifically, Nietzsche thinks there is a *looping effect* between the psychological disposition named by a character trait-term and the practice of using that term. While he affirms that people are differentially disposed to certain patterns of behavior (because of differences in the strength and configuration of their instincts and other drives), he conceives of these dispositions as fluid both in their objects and, to a lesser degree, in their strength and aim. Someone disposed to the activity of inquiry will end up thinking, feeling, and acting very differently depending on whether he is labeled "curious" or "nosy." Someone disposed toward aggression will end up thinking, feeling, and acting very differently depending on whether he is considered a hero or a criminal (TI "Skirmishes" 45). The valence and content of the labels applied to an agent, together with the power-relation between the labeler and labeled, interact with her underlying psychological dispositions to

---

[7] Riccardi (2021) illuminatingly discusses the role of community in Nietzsche's philosophy of mind, tying it in particular to the herd instinct.

produce the kind of person she eventually becomes. This phenomenon is perhaps most clearly articulated in D 38:

> The same drive evolves into the painful feeling of *cowardice* under the impress of the reproach custom has imposed upon this drive: or into the pleasant feeling of *humility* if it happens that a custom such as the Christian has taken it to its heart and called it *good*. That is to say, it is attended by either a good or a bad conscience! In itself it has, *like every drive*, neither this moral character nor any moral character at all, nor even a definite attendant sensation of pleasure or displeasure: it acquires all this, as its second nature, only when it enters into relations with drives already baptized good or evil.

How someone's drives develop and express themselves depends on the semantics and valence of the labels applied to them. Moreover, as people's dispositions shift under the impress of labels, the meaning of the labels themselves evolves. If nobility is whatever noble people are disposed to think, feel, and do, then when noble people's psychological dispositions change, so too does the meaning of nobility (and of "nobility"). Preexisting psychological drives and other dispositions are shaped by the activity of labeling, which in turn modulates the meaning of the label, which further shapes the psychological disposition, and so on in a dynamic feedback loop.

For Nietzsche, there are two distinct styles of becoming what one is called: the social and the reflexive. Someone whose character is built according to the social plan becomes what others consider and call him – good, bad, or mixed. Nietzsche associates this blueprint for the construction of character with slavishness. By contrast, someone whose character is built according to the reflexive plan becomes what she considers and calls herself. Nietzsche associates this method of character construction with masterliness. It will turn out, however, that the masterly path is itself social – and in multiple ways.

Higher-Order Types

Unlike Aristotle, who thinks that one becomes virtuous through practice and habituation, realizing all the while that one is not yet virtuous but aiming to become so, Nietzsche thinks that the temporal relation sometimes runs in the other direction. First, one supposes, imagines, hopes, or is told that one is a certain way – that one has certain character traits. One projects this image of oneself into the social world, and sometimes secures uptake. Or, this image is projected onto one and accepted. Either way, one becomes committed to a standard of conduct that includes not only one's actions but also one's thoughts, feelings, emotions, and deliberative strategies. Commitment to this standard in turn induces congruent behavior. Thus, thinking of oneself as having certain traits is temporally and conceptually prior to actually having those traits. This is a theme that crops up especially in the *Genealogy*, where Nietzsche describes the nobles not so much as being psychologically higher but as imagining themselves to be higher psychologically because they are already politically higher (GM I:3, 3.14). This imagination induces (enough of) them to behave as if they were higher, which has knock-on social effects that lead to self-confirmatory conduct. This theme also crops up, in a less uplifting way, in his description of psychological slavishness – a disposition to simulate, mimic, or acquire whatever character traits are attributed to one. Instead of or in addition to feeling committed to a certain code of conduct, the slavish person feels that other people, especially others with the power to impose sanctions and punishments, expect him to behave in accordance with a certain code of conduct. Thus, while both psychological masters and psychological slaves become what they are taken to be, the masters do so by becoming what they take themselves to be, whereas the psychologically slavish become what others take them to be.

Social Character Construction

At first blush, it may seem most natural to categorize a trait attribution as an assertion: to say that someone is T is to commit oneself to the truth of the proposition that the person has the disposition in question. Compare attributions of other dispositions, such as, "This table is flammable," and, "You conduct electricity." The former commits the speaker to the truth of the proposition that the table would burn in certain conditions; the latter commits the speaker to the truth of the proposition that the hearer would conduct free electrons in certain conditions. Why should attributions of psychological dispositions be any different? Yet Nietzsche thinks that it may be more apt to interpret trait attributions as directives or declarations because they either cause the hearer to engage in a certain type of behavior or make it the case that they are true by being felicitously uttered.

It's straightforward to see how a trait attribution might be used as a directive. If someone is organizing a workshop and I say within Mandi's earshot, "Mandi is quite reliable when it comes to making plans. Let's ask her to help with the organization!" it's plausible to suppose that I am not too subtly goading her into helping with the planning and following through on her commitments. Nietzsche thinks that trait attributions are sometimes used in this way to summon virtues (or ersatz virtues that are actually vices), as he indicates in GS 21:

> A man's virtues are called *good* depending on their probable consequences not for him but for us and society: the praise of virtues has always been far from "selfless," far from "unegoistic." Otherwise one would have had to notice that virtues (like industriousness, obedience, chastity, filial piety, and justice) are usually harmful for those who possess them, being instincts that dominate them too violently and covetously and resist the efforts of reason to keep them in balance with their other instincts. [...] But your neighbor praises your virtue precisely on this account.

However, this is only one way of making trait attributions. It is less obvious that a trait attribution might function as a declaration; this is Nietzsche's innovation. Standard examples of declarations are baptisms ("I hereby christen this ship the 'Titanic'") and institutional acts of labeling ("I hereby pronounce you married"). One of the odd things about these speech acts is their direction-of-fit. The ship is called "Titanic" because it was thus christened; it is not christened "Titanic" because that is what it is called. The couple is married because they have been so pronounced; they were not so pronounced because they were married.

Nietzsche thinks that many people have the character traits they do in part because they have been labeled with those traits; in other words, some trait attributions are declarations. This would be a special case of his insight that "what things *are called* is incomparably more important than what they are" because the "reputation, name, and appearance, the usual measure and weight of a thing, what it counts for [...] grows to be part of the thing and turns into its very body" (GS 58). He claims, for instance, that "from time immemorial, in all strata of people who are in some way dependent, base people *were* only what they were *considered to be*." Perception comes before perceived when the perceived have no sense of themselves or their value: "not being at all accustomed to positing values, the only value the base person attributes to himself is the one his masters have attributed to him (creating values is the true *right of masters*)" (BGE 261).

Nietzsche's idea is that those of lower rank take on not only the tasks and jobs but also the character traits that are attributed to them. They become, quite literally, what they are called. As he puts it in GS 356:

> The need to make a living still forces nearly all European men to adopt a particular role – their so-called profession. A few retain the freedom, an apparent freedom, to choose this role for themselves; for most of them it is chosen. The result is strange enough. Almost all Europeans, at an advanced age, confuse themselves with their role; they become the victims of their 'good performance' [....] Upon deeper consideration, the role has actually *become* character; and artifice, nature.

If slavish people are labeled "dishonest," they become dishonest. If they are labeled "cowardly," they become cowardly. If they are labeled "ambitious," they become ambitious.

Here we begin to see a cleavage between the political and the psychological senses of slavishness. Politically, to be a slave is to have one's will subordinated, to be in another's power; psychologically, to be a slave is to be disposed to think, feel, and act as expected. While it would not be incorrect to say that Nietzsche is more concerned with the psychological than the political, he is most interested in their interaction. He thinks that almost everyone in modern culture has inherited some degree of psychological slavishness. Because so many of our ancestors were considered slaves (i.e., were politically enslaved), they acquired or developed psychological slavishness, which they then passed on to us as the herd instinct. Through a "tremendous atavism," even today "ordinary people still *wait* for an opinion to be pronounced about themselves before instinctively deferring to it. And this is by no means only the case with 'good' opinions – they defer to bad and unfair ones as well" (BGE 261).

Being treated as a person of a certain type can have profound effects, especially when the treatment begins at birth and is presented as part of the natural order of things. So, for example, Nietzsche says that "at bottom the masses are willing to submit to slavery of any kind, if only the higher-ups constantly legitimize themselves as higher, as *born* to command" (GS 40). And in GS 52, he remarks that, "What we know about ourselves and remember is not as decisive to our life's happiness as it is believed to be." Instead, he goes on to suggest, "One day, what *others* know (or think they know) about us assails us – and then we realize that that is more powerful. It is easier to deal with a bad conscience than a bad reputation."

This process need not be carried out at the level of consciousness. Instead, even slavish people think that they are acting in their own interest and from their own character. But "what they do is done for the phantom of their ego which has formed itself in the heads of those around them and has been communicated to them [...] the one forever in the head of someone else, and the head of this someone else again in the heads of others" (D 105). After taking a label to heart, they act in accordance with it. This leads others, as well as they themselves, to think the label was aptly applied in the first place. It also reinforces their first-order disposition to behave in accordance with the label. After many cycles of such pretense, social confirmation, and habit formation, the trait becomes second nature. By pretending to be what one is designated, one becomes what one is designated. As Nietzsche puts it, "The hypocrite who always plays one and the same role finally ceases to be a hypocrite [. . . .] If someone obstinately and for a long time wants to *appear* something it is in the end hard for him to *be* anything else" (HH 51). He makes a similar point in D 248, which is titled "*Dissimulation as a duty.*" "Goodness," Nietzsche says, "has mostly been developed by the protracted dissimulation which sought to appear as goodness." For this reason, "The lie is, if not the mother, then the nurse of goodness. Honesty has likewise been reared mostly by the requirement to seem honest: it happened within the hereditary aristocracies. What is dissimulated for a long time at last becomes *nature*: dissimulation in the end sublimates itself, and organs and instincts are the surprising fruit of the garden of hypocrisy." In the garden of hypocrisy, types are cultivated and fine-tuned until people's instincts count as (and are) virtues, such as honesty. Likewise, Nietzsche attributes to the priestly type (and also to the philosophical type) "the art of *falling for your own forgeries*" (A 12), though we shall see below that this is more masterly than slavish.

What leads people to act out of a slavish second-order disposition? Social fear. For example, in D 104, Nietzsche argues that fear is essential to understanding this phenomenon:

> All actions may be traced back to evaluations, all evaluations are either *original* or *adopted* – the latter being by far the most common. Why do we adopt them? From fear – that is to say, we consider it more advisable to pretend they are our own – and accustom ourself to this pretense, so that at length it becomes our own nature.

In this passage, Nietzsche claims that the vast majority of people's evaluations are foisted on them by their society and culture. Fear also plays a prominent role in BGE 201, where Nietzsche distinguishes fear of outsiders during intergroup conflict and fear of members of one's own community when security against outsiders has been attained. In the latter cases,

> certain strong and dangerous drives such as enterprise, daring, vindictiveness, cunning, rapacity, and a dominating spirit must have been not only honored (under different names than these of course), but nurtured and cultivated (since, given the threats to the group, they were constantly needed against the common enemies). Now, however, since there are no more escape valves for these drives, they are seen as twice as dangerous and, one by one, are denounced as immoral.

These drives, suggests Nietzsche, do not disappear when they are rebaptized as vices. Instead, people become what they are called. When their instincts and other drives are diabolized, they become criminals.

Ordinary first-order dispositions like flammability do not depend on higher-order dispositions. On Nietzsche's view, first-order psychological dispositions sometimes do. And this dependence has both ontogenetic and phylogenetic aspects. Most of our ancestors were politically enslaved to some extent, which led the majority of them to become psychologically slavish. We have inherited this second-order disposition, and we express and reinforce it whenever we become what we are called.

Reflexive Character Construction

The social blueprint for the construction of character relies on a kind of psychological receptivity. To become what one is called, one must be to some extent disposed to acquire or simulate whatever traits are attributed to one, to bend one's drives to the model of the traits one is expected to embody. To be evaluated, one must be evaluable. The other side of the coin is the disposition to assign value, to evaluate. This is what Nietzsche often has in mind when he speaks not of political but of psychological masterliness or nobility. This disposition enables one to see oneself in a positive light, and to project confidence in that self-image (GS 78).

One of Nietzsche's most sustained treatments of the moral psychology of nobility is the first essay of GM. There, he claims, against the "English psychologists" that the judgment 'good' did *not* originate with those to whom 'goodness' was shown! Rather it was 'the good' themselves, that is to say, the noble, powerful, high-stationed, and high-minded, who felt and established themselves and their actions as good, that is, of the first rank, in contradistinction to all the low, low-minded, common, and plebian. (GM I:2)

Unlike the slaves, these nobles are what they say they are (because that's what they say they are). Their self-evaluations are declarations, not assertions or directives. Nietzsche even speculates that "the origin of language itself [is] an expression of power on the part of the rulers: they say 'this *is* this and this'" (GM I:2). Whereas the political underclass becomes psychologically slavish, and is thus molded from the outside, members of the nobility practice reflexive evaluation.

Even with the nobles, though, there is a shift from the political to the psychological. They begin by celebrating their social dominance, but end in an affirmation of their own character traits. This is the "*conceptual transformation*" that Nietzsche describes in GM I:4, saying that "everywhere 'noble,' 'aristocratic' in the social sense, is the basic concept from which 'good' in the sense of 'with aristocratic soul,' 'noble,' 'with a soul of high order,' 'with a privileged soul' necessarily developed." Their political superiority engenders the confidence to affirm their own drives, which they subsequently take to be responsible for that very superiority (GM I:6). But this shift presupposes that the nobles, too, are not already, but rather become, what they say they are. Their virtues are acquired through self-labeling. Like the slaves, they have a second-order receptivity: They are disposed to acquire whatever dispositions are attributed to them by themselves.

This is just one of the paradoxical features of psychological masterliness. Another is the extent to which it, too, is grounded in social relations and processes. As I have presented it thus far, it might seem that the reflexive model of character development is extremely individualistic. A masterly person self-attributes some character traits, which she then goes on to acquire. But this is not how Nietzsche envisions the process. No individual has that much control. The content of most masterly self-attributions is social in multiple ways. First, the form of such an attribution tends to be not, "I am noble," but, "We are noble." We – this community of people to which I belong – share this virtue. The self-attribution thus relies on there being a social group to which the individual belongs. Second, the content of the trait-term tends to be social as well. Nobility or being noble is itself perhaps the best example of this phenomenon. It implies a community of respect and honor, in which each member expects certain kinds of thoughts, feelings, and behaviors from the rest. "As one who is good, one belongs to the 'good,' a community that possesses a communal feeling because all individuals are knit together by the sense of repayment" (HH 45).

Still another way in which even the reflexive blueprint for the construction of character is grounded in social relations and processes is that, like many declarations, self-attributions require acceptance or uptake from the audience. The ship is called "Titanic" because someone christens it "Titanic," but the christening is felicitous only because the audience accepts the declaration. The couple is married because they have been so pronounced, but the pronouncement only succeeds because the audience accepts it. Someone who declares, "We are noble" is noble, but only because the declaration is accepted. To be noble, they need to be considered noble – by themselves, by other nobles, and even by the slaves. So "aristocratic *culture* breathes power, and if its customs very often demand merely the semblance of the feeling of power, the impression this game produces on the non-aristocratic, and the spectacle of this impression, nonetheless constantly enhance the actual feeling of superiority" (D 201).

Yet another way in which the reflexive blueprint for the construction of character is grounded in social relations and processes is that it sometimes involves the temporally extended and externalized process of falling for one's own forgeries (A 12). In the moment of self-attribution, a noble individual may realize that what they're saying about themselves is false or a kind of bullshit. However, by projecting that message into the world and having it echoed back to them by credulous others, they gain confidence in their forgery (BGE 148). One striking example of this process is in GM III:10, where Nietzsche says that the

> earliest philosophers knew how to endow their existence with a meaning [. . .] through which others might come to *fear* them: more closely considered, they did so from an even more fundamental need, namely so as to fear and reverence themselves. For they found all the value judgments within them turned *against* them, they had to fight down every kind of suspicion and resistance against 'the philosopher in them'.

These early philosophers were in danger of running afoul of the evaluative integration constraint on virtue. They were in a position of condemning their own drives. In order to secure a good conscience for themselves, they projected a false image into the world that was met with fear and reverence, which they themselves then internalized, thus forging unity in an otherwise shattered breast. Nietzsche goes on to characterize this socio-emotional self-therapy as typical of philosophers:

> The philosophical spirit always had to use as a mask and cocoon the *previously established* types of the contemplative man – priest, sorcerer, soothsayer, and in any case a religious type – in order to be able to *exist at all: the ascetic ideal* for a long time served the philosopher as a form in which to appear, as a precondition of existence – he had to *represent* it so as to be able to be a philosopher; he had to *believe* in it in order to be able to represent it. (GM III:15)

Once again, we see pretense that gets echoed back to the pretender as sincerity and then reinternalized.

5 Nietzsche's Virtues

Virtue depends on both agentic integration and evaluative integration. Agentic integration is a matter of getting one's instincts and other drives to get out of each other's way (weak integration) or mutually support each other (strong integration), which can be achieved in various ways, such as shaping their expression or upregulating or downregulating them – though they are only malleable within limits. Evaluative integration is a matter of accepting and even embracing fixed aspects of oneself. In other words, evaluative integration is a matter of accepting and even embracing instincts and other drives that cannot be shaped or regulated any longer or any further.

In order to achieve these two types of integration, you would have to be either lucky or self-knowledgeable, especially if you embody a complex set of drives. You can't just assume that your type, your constellation of drives, is the same as the most-common or the most-praised in your society. Doing so may lead you to try to live a life that you are fundamentally incapable of living, leading either to the wrecking of your agency or to your being wracked by shame and guilt.

Furthermore, because evaluative integration depends so heavily on social acceptance and affirmation, knowing one's culture, choosing one's culture, and criticizing and changing one's culture are essential to leading a good life. Wayfinding through life without self-knowledge and knowledge of one's culture and available alternatives to it is like going to sea without a nautical map, or with an antiquated map made for different sailors on different seas. You might reach your destination safely, but the odds are against it.

Likewise, navigating relationships without knowledge of others' types, their constellations of drives, is bound to lead to conflict, disappointment, or tyrannical demands. It's like expecting a fox to guard your henhouse, a rabbit to help you hunt wolves, or a tired old horse to pull a cart that is too heavy for it. Consider an example: you're at a party with a friend with whom you've had sex before, and they express interest in going home with you but at the last second decide to sleep with someone else. Regardless of who they end up with, their drives are the same, but they are expressed in different ways. If someone is impulsive and sexually curious, and those drives are fundamental to their nature, then expecting anything else from them is a demand for them to compromise their agency or to endure emotional turmoil or torment. To the extent that you genuinely value a person, you have to accept how their drives, especially their strong fixed drives, get expressed, whether to your benefit or to your chagrin. To say no to the latter is implicitly to say no to the former, which amounts to a rejection of the other person's individuality, to precisely what you ought to treasure in them if you are going to enjoy a relationship worth having.

For these reasons, our flourishing is to a large extent contingent on our knowledge – of ourselves, of the other people in our lives, and of our culture and the available alternatives to it. For people who happen to embody a strong inquisitive drive, this drive thus turns out to be extremely valuable. If you are curious and if you can direct your curiosity to your own type, to the types of the people in your life, and to your culture and its available alternatives, then you might just be able to plot, tentatively and stage by stage, a happy course through life that you can authentically affirm. In this section, I argue that this is why Nietzsche embraces a range of epistemic virtues, especially for those who share his type, namely curiosity, solitude, intellectual courage, and having a sense of humor. Curiosity fosters (among other things) self-knowledge, while solitude fosters critical knowledge of one's community. Since acquiring such knowledge of the less savory aspects of the *I* and the *we* can be deeply aversive, curiosity and solitude need to be supported by the executive virtues of intellectual courage and having a sense of humor. Intellectual courage helps one to overcome the fear associated with inquiry, while having a sense of humor enables one to maintain positive affect while recognizing unpleasant truths and giving up cherished illusions.

Curiosity

Nietzsche doesn't have much to say about reliability as contemporary epistemologists understand it. This may be a good thing, as there are strong arguments against the reliability criterion for knowledge literature (Turri 2015). Lani Watson (2018) in particular has persuasively argued that, even if other intellectual virtues must be reliably successful, curiosity needn't. What makes curiosity a virtue is instead the way it helps us latch onto and sink our teeth into interesting questions. There is something worthwhile in being a "seeker after knowledge" (HH 630), as Reginster (2013, 2015) emphasizes. Curiosity entails a delight in the "danger of uncertainty" (GS "Pref"). Nietzschean curiosity finds value in the activity of confronting uncertainty through inquiry. For instance, in HL 6, he praises a peculiar form of epistemic justice because "the highest and rarest virtues are united and concealed in justice." Someone who embodies this virtue "tries to ascend from indulgent doubt to stern certainty." Embodying such a trait, though, is difficult; for some it may be impossible. And, it is therefore the near-hopeless pursuit of epistemic justice that qualifies one as "the most *venerable* exemplar of the species man." Cristy (2019) offers a similar interpretation of Nietzsche on epistemic justice.

In D 270, Nietzsche characterizes scientific pursuit as "the strict conscience for what is true and actual," "a greedy longing for knowledge," and "a duty to desire to be present as a witness *wherever* knowledge is present and to let nothing already known escape again." In D 327, he paints a portrait of a Don Giovanni of spirit, who "does not love the things he knows, but has spirit and appetite for and enjoyment of the chase and intrigues of knowledge – up to the highest and remotest stars of knowledge!" This same idea crops up in D 396: "This one is hunting pleasant truths, that one unpleasant. But even the former takes more pleasure in the hunt than in the booty." Next, in D 424 Nietzsche echoes this idea, saying, "In earlier times [. . .] the conviction that mankind was the goal of nature was so strong that it was assumed without question that nothing could be disclosed by knowledge that was not salutary and useful to man, indeed that things other than this *could* not, *ought* not to *exist*." Now, however, we recognize that there are such terrible truths, and people driven by curiosity find them especially tantalizing objects of inquiry.

In D 429 Nietzsche makes it clear that the kind of curiosity he's discussing is distinctively associated with his own type: "Our *drive to knowledge*," he says, "has become too strong for us to be able to want happiness without knowledge or the happiness of a strong, firmly rooted delusion." He goes on: "Restless discovering and divining has such an attraction for us, and has grown as indispensable to us [. . . .] Knowledge has in us been transformed into a passion which shrinks at no sacrifice and at bottom fears nothing but its own extinction." As before, curiosity here is best understood as a "restless" drive to engage in inquiry.

Turning now to *The Gay Science*, we find several passages that further elucidate the nature of Nietzschean curiosity. In GS "Pref" 2, while speaking of his own convalescence, Nietzsche says, "A psychologist knows few questions as attractive as that concerning the relation between health and philosophy; and should he himself become ill, he will bring all of his scientific curiosity into the illness."

In GS 249, Nietzsche returns to the insatiability of the drive to inquire. He describes "the passion of coming to know" as a kind of "greed" for experience, including empathetic engagement from multiple points of view ("to see with the eyes and seize with the hands of many individuals"). In GS 351, he claims that some philosophers are distinguished by a peculiar drive: "the great *passion* of the knowledge-seeker who steadfastly lives, must live, in the thundercloud of the highest problems and the weightiest responsibilities." Someone possessed of this passion does not assume that he already possesses the truth. On the contrary, he presupposes that there are many important truths that he does not yet know, and this motivates his inquiry. Thus, Nietzsche says, "It was *modesty* that in Greece coined the word 'philosopher' and left the extraordinary insolence of calling oneself wise to the actors of the spirit [the sophists]." Next, in GS 375, Nietzsche describes the epistemic attitude characteristic of his own type as "the gleeful curiosity of the one who used to stand in the corner and was driven to despair by his corner and who now delights and luxuriates in the opposite of a corner." The metaphor of the corner suggests a single, cramped perspective, whereas the "opposite of a corner" must refer to a wide-open space in which one can roam and try out a variety of perspectives. Someone driven to such roaming, says Nietzsche, "will not easily let go of the questionable character of things," and stays in control "as our urge for certainty races ahead."

In GS 382, while discussing the dispositions needed by exemplars of his own type, Nietzsche says, "Anyone whose soul thirsts to experience the whole range of previous values and aspirations, to sail around all the coasts of this 'inland sea' of ideals, anyone who wants to know from the adventures of his own experience how it feels to be the discoverer or conqueror of an ideal" needs "*the great health*," which makes them robust against the psychological tribulations they're likely to encounter in their inquiries. Those lucky enough to enjoy such health face an as yet undiscovered land the boundaries of which no one has yet surveyed, beyond all the lands and corners of the ideal heretofore, a world so over-rich in what is beautiful, strange, questionable, terrible, and divine that our curiosity and our thirst to possess it have veered beyond control.

In this passage, Nietzsche self-attributes insatiable curiosity. This drive to inquiry is expressed by adopting a wide range of evaluative perspectives.

In the publications of 1886, Nietzsche continued to engage with and self-attribute curiosity. We can see this both in the preface material added to *Human, All-Too-Human* and in *Beyond Good and Evil*. The preface material is explicitly self-reflective. Nietzsche here takes stock of what he has accomplished, what he has experienced, and what he has become. First, in HH "Pref" 3, he describes what he calls the "great liberation." This is a sort of road-to-Damascus moment for those who previously felt a robust sense of duty and obligation. During the great liberation, this was discussed and quoted at length earlier. Consider what the person experiencing the great liberation does next: "With a wicked laugh he turns round whatever he finds veiled [. . .]: he puts to the test what these things look like *when* they are reversed. [. . . He is] full of curiosity and the desire to tempt and experiment." In the next passage (HH "Pref" 4), Nietzsche says that, after this great liberation, one who does not fall apart psychologically may experience "a pale, subtle happiness of light and sunshine, a feeling of bird-like freedom, bird-like altitude, bird-like exuberance, and a third thing in which curiosity is united with a tender contempt" which enables him to use "even wickedness as a means and fish-hook of knowledge."

The preface added to the *Assorted Opinions and Maxims* is similar. For example, in HH AOM "Pref" 1, Nietzsche describes *Human, All-Too-Human* "As a book 'for free spirits,'" saying that "there reposes upon it something of the almost cheerful and curious coldness of the psychologist who takes a host of painful things that lie *beneath* and *behind* him and identifies and as it were *impales* them with the point of a needle." Likewise, in HH AOM "Pref" 4, Nietzsche describes his own past as a process of taking "sides *against* myself." He follows this up in HH AOM "Pref" 5 by saying, "It was only then that I learned that solitary's speech that only the most silent and the most suffering understand [. . . .] It was then I learned the art of *appearing* cheerful, objective, curious, above all healthy and malicious." This reversal in affective orienta-tion served, according to Nietzsche, both as a buffer to his psychological health and as an epistemic methodology: "I, as physician and patient in one, compelled myself to an opposite and unexplored *clime of the soul* [from the pessimism that dominated him previously], and especially to a curative jour-ney into strange parts, into *strangeness* itself, to a curiosity regarding every kind of strange thing."

Turning to *Beyond Good and Evil*, in BGE 26 Nietzsche contends that, "The long and serious study of the *average* man [is] a necessary part of the life story of every philosopher." But, he admits, such study is difficult both because it involves so much effort and because it involves so much disgust and disappointment. The saving grace is that, if he is lucky, the philosopher will find real shortcuts and aids to make his work easier. I mean he will find so-called cynics – people who easily recognize the animal, the commonplace, the 'norm' within themselves, and yet still have a degree of spiritedness and an urge to talk about themselves and their peers *in front of witnesses*.

It is for this reason that "the higher man needs to open his ears to all cynicism, crude or refined, and congratulate himself every time the buffoon speaks up without shame, or the scientific satyr is heard right in front of him." The gregarious cynic is an instrument in the hands of the empathic moral psychologist; he makes it possible to see how the world and humanity appear from an especially inhospitable evaluative point of view.

In BGE 44, Nietzsche concludes his chapter on the free spirit. In this passage, he explicitly distinguishes between a "we" (the free spirits) and a "they" (the new philosophers), then goes on to blur the line between them by attributing many of the same dispositions to both groups. Of the free spirits, he says,

> [a]t home in many countries of the spirit, at least as guests; repeatedly slipping away from the musty, comfortable corners where preference and prejudice, youth, origin, accidents of people and books, and even the fatigue of traveling seem to have driven us [...] grateful even for difficulties and inconstant health, because they have always freed us from some rule and its "prejudice," grateful to god, devil, sheep, and maggot in us, curious to a fault, researchers to the point of cruelty, with unmindful fingers for the incomprehensible, with teeth and stomachs for the indigestible, ready for any trade that requires a quick wit and sharp senses, ready for any risk [....] This is the type of people we are!

What I want to focus on here is which specific virtues Nietzsche is summoning in this passage. There is a contrast between the dogmatic perspective of the "comfortable corner" and the ranging, dynamic perspectivism that is "at home" or at least a "guest" in many affective and evaluative points of view. These points of view include both good and bad health, which make it possible to see things in radically different lights. Doing so enables those of Nietzsche's type ("we free spirits") to engage and express their curiosity. In the next passage (BGE 45), Nietzsche makes a self-ascription: "A curiosity of my type remains the most agreeable of all vices; – oh sorry! I meant to say: the love of truth finds its reward in heaven and even on earth."

In BGE 214, the first section of the "Our virtues" chapter of *Beyond Good and Evil*, Nietzsche claims that his type of person has a distinctive set of virtue: with all our dangerous curiosity, our diversity and art of disguises, our worn-out and, as it were, saccharine cruelty in sense and in spirit, – *if* we happen to have virtues, they will presumably only be the ones that have learned best how to get along with our most secret and heartful propensities.

Here Nietzsche gives expression to the internal harmony required for a drive to be a virtue. In people of his type, he says, curiosity and various other virtues "get along with" the agent's propensities and desires – that is to say, with their other drives.

Later, in BGE 227 Nietzsche suggests that "genuine honesty" is one of the virtues characteristic of free spirits, that it is "our virtue and we cannot get rid of it."[8] Recall that in Nietzsche's framework, someone's drives are fluid but only within certain bounds. Given this state of psychological affairs, he recommends contextualizing honesty with a variety of other dispositions: "We will help it out with whatever devilishness we have – our disgust at clumsiness and approximation, our '*nitimur in vetitum*,' our adventurer's courage, our sly and discriminating curiosity."

Finally, in BGE 292, Nietzsche describes the philosopher as a "type" of person "who constantly experiences, sees, hears, suspects, hopes, and dreams extraordinary things; who is struck by his own thoughts as if from outside," and "who is frequently running away from himself, frequently afraid of himself, – but too curious not to always come back to himself."

Nietzsche continues to engage with the virtue of curiosity in the *Genealogy of Morals*. First, in GM "Pref" 3 he characterizes himself as having a specific set of dispositions: "a scruple peculiar to me" that guaranteed that "my curiosity as well as my suspicions were bound to halt quite soon at the question of where our good and evil really *originated*." Second, in GM III:9 he ascribes a range of activities, proclivities, and drives to himself and those of his type:

> We experiment with ourselves in a way we would never permit ourselves to experiment with animals and, carried away by curiosity, we cheerfully vivisect our souls [. . . .] We violate ourselves nowadays, no doubt of it, we nutcrackers of the soul, ever questioning and questionable, as if life were nothing but cracking nuts; and thus we are bound to grow day-by-day more questionable, *worthier* of asking questions; perhaps also worthier – of living?

In both of these passages, Nietzsche describes himself as an inquisitor who wants to know about the origins of (judgments of) good and evil. He wants to learn in ways that are tantamount to self-torture.

Lastly, let's turn to *Ecce Homo*. In EH "Clever" 1, Nietzsche brags that he has never been able to take theological concepts seriously, then claims that, for him, atheism "is an instinct. I have too much curiosity, too many doubts and high

---

[8] Huddleston (2019, p. 38) also points to BGE 39 as a passage in which Nietzsche praises the sort of honesty that leads one to recognize hard truths.

spirits to be happy with a ridiculously crude answer. God is a ridiculously crude answer." Nietzsche's inborn curiosity is an example of the sort of instinct that can – at least in some types of people in some communities – constitute a virtue. Next, in EH "Books" 3, Nietzsche tells us what sort of person he wants as a reader: "When I imagine a perfect reader, I always think of a monster of courage and curiosity who is also supple, cunning, cautious, a born adventurer and discoverer." Nietzsche is not simply telling us what his ideal reader is like. He is inviting (some of) his readers to find these traits in themselves and to start expressing them.

Solitude

Whereas curiosity is a drive to inquire that often leads to self-knowledge, including knowledge of unpleasant attributes of the *I*, solitude is a drive to inquire that often leads to knowledge of unpleasant attributes of the *we*, especially of one's community, and even more especially of one's unelective affiliations such as family and nation. Given the constitutive role that community plays in the construction of virtue, such knowledge is indispensable, and it can be achieved by those who embody the drive that Nietzsche calls solitude [*Einsamkeit*].

For Nietzsche, solitude is closely linked with the figure of the hermit and the figure of the wanderer. The hermit [*Einseidler*] shows up in thirty-four distinct passages in the published and authorized manuscripts. The wanderer [*Wanderer*] turns up in twenty-seven distinct passages in the published and authorized manuscripts. Historically, the hermit's traditional way of life resembles Nietzschean solitude in central ways. While Nietzsche does not specifically mention Simeon Stylites in any of these passages, he presumably has figures like Simeon in mind when he writes about hermits and other adherents of the ascetic ideal in the third essay of the *Genealogy of Morals*. Simeon in particular is an interesting exemplar because, even though he lived apart and above – on a small platform atop a pillar – he was not banished or completely alienated from his community. Instead, he voluntarily placed himself adjacent to and above it. In addition, Simeon was respected by his local community, many members of which were awed by his bizarre asceticism and came to him as advice-seekers (Adamson 2015). Nietzsche remarks on the function of such bizarre self-denial in HH 141, saying that "The Christian practical pessimists had [. . .] an interest in seeing that" erotic love was conceived as intrinsically bad because "they required for their solitude [. . .] an enemy always on the alert: an enemy, moreover, that was universally recognized through the combating and overcoming of whom they could repeatedly appear to the non-saints as half-incomprehensible, supernatural beings." The Nietzschean cultural critic uses his emotional solitude in similar ways. Though he aims to do so without adopting a life-denying stance, he nevertheless adopts a pose of being adjacent to and above his in-group, and he expects members of that in-group to seek his criticism and advice.

In SE 3, Nietzsche argues that Schopenhauer "was a total solitary." He goes on to claim that "No one who possesses true friends knows what true solitude is, even though he have the whole world around him for his enemies. – Ah, I well understand that you do not know what solitude is." The implication is that Nietzsche himself does know what solitude is. The passage continues with the suggestion that philosophers and other people who have fled inward for their freedom also have to live outwardly, become visible, let themselves be seen; they are united with mankind through countless ties of blood, residence, education, fatherland, chance, the importunity of others; they are likewise presupposed to harbor countless opinions simply because these are the ruling opinions of the time

Solitude is the virtue that enables and even drives its bearer to contravene these presuppositions, to deny in-group defaults.

In *Human, All-Too-Human,* Nietzsche continues his reflections on solitude. In HH 142, he says that "the saint practices that defiance of oneself that is a close relation of lust for power and bestows the feeling of power even upon the solitary." He develops this idea further elsewhere – especially in the second and third essays of the *Genealogy,* where he analyzes this drive to self-defiance as the instinct of cruelty turned inward and labels it the "bad conscience." Later, in HH 282, Nietzsche argues that because nowadays "time for thinking and quietness in thinking are lacking, one no longer ponders deviant views." This should strike us as similar to his distaste for uncritically accepting the default ways of life and thinking in one's community or in-group. Here, the virtue of solitude is associated with both cultural critique and advice-giving. The solitary free spirit is able to deviate in thought and feeling from the local norms of his in-group. In this way, he is able to diagnose and direct reforms of the flaws that others in his community are too close to see.

HH 282 also suggests that the emotional position of solitude is ambivalent. Someone could be isolated because they have been cast out, exiled, or banished. Alternatively, someone could be isolated because they have chosen, temporarily, to remove themselves from their community in order to get a better perspective on it. The Nietzschean virtue of solitude is associated with the latter emotional point of view. We find examples of this idea in both HH 625 and HH 638. In the former, Nietzsche says that "Some men are so accustomed to being alone with themselves that they do not compare themselves with others at all but spin out their life of monologue in a calm and cheerful mood, conversing and indeed laughing with themselves alone." According to Nietzsche, such men tend to be unfair to themselves when they do make social comparisons, so we should "allow certain men their solitude and not be so stupid, as we often are, as to pity them for it." In HH 638, Nietzsche begins by saying that "He who has attained to only some degree of freedom of mind cannot feel other than a wanderer on the earth – though not as a traveler *to* a final destination: for this destination does not exist." Nietzsche goes on to say that the wanderer's life can be hard, but that it has its own distinctive rewards. In this passage, Nietzsche suggests that solitude fosters companionship among people of the same type, who share values and expectations. In the wilderness, one is not pressured and presumed to accept the orthodoxies of the community assigned to one by the lottery of birth and upbringing. This makes it possible to forge a very different sort of bond: elective affinity with those who share one's values.

If we turn next to the prefaces added to *Human, All-Too-Human* in 1886, we find Nietzsche congratulating himself for writing books that "contain snares and nets for unwary birds and in effect a persistent invitation to the overturning of habitual evaluations and valued habits." He then goes on to describe his own "profound suspiciousness" about his community's values and heroes, as well as "the fears and frosts of the isolation to which that unconditional *disparity of view*" condemns him (HH "Pref" 1). Just two sections later, Nietzsche describes the "great liberation" of the youthful soul. Among the other emotional upheavals that characterize the great liberation are "contempt for what is called 'duty'" and "a rebellious arbitrary, volcanically erupting desire for travel, strange places, estrangements, coldness, soberness, frost." Eventually, says Nietzsche, "Solitude encircles him, ever more threatening, suffocating, heart-tightening, that terrible goddess and *mater saeva cupidinum* – but who today knows what *solitude* is?" Nietzsche suggests in the next passage (HH "Pref" 4) that he himself does: "From this morbid isolation, from the desert of these years of temptation and experiment, it is still a long road to that tremendous over-flowing certainty and health." Solitude is the drive to get emotionally away from and above one's community, one's home; it is a sort of instinctual aversion to the familiar and attraction to the strange and new. In HH AOM "Pref" 4 Nietzsche also describes his own solitude, claiming that, in order to regain "that courage-ous pessimism that is the antithesis of all romantic mendacity," he entered a psychological state of being "lonely and sorely mistrustful of myself" in which he "took sides *against* myself and *for* everything painful and difficult precisely for *me*."

In the preface added to *Daybreak*, Nietzsche makes it clear that solitude is a virtue only for those who share his type. Addressing himself to his readers in

D "Pref" 2 as "my patient friends," he says, "I shall now tell you what I was after down there [...] Do not think for a moment that I intend to invite you to the same hazardous enterprise! Or even only to the same solitude!" In what did this solitary path consist? Nietzsche tells us: "I commenced an investigation and digging out of an ancient *faith*, one upon which we philosophers have for a couple of millennia been accustomed to build as if upon the firmest of all foundations [...] our *faith in morality*." In this passage, we see solitude allying with curiosity: The further Nietzsche's inquiries take him, the more solitude he feels. And these inquiries are into the comfortable and comforting truisms of his community, what Procrustean moralists have been "accustomed to build" upon.

The epistemic value of solitude crops up elsewhere in *Daybreak*. For example, in D 114, Nietzsche suggests that "intellectual benefit" accrues to anyone who experiences "profound solitude." But solitude's value is not only epistemic. It also contributes to emotional well-being. In a brief aphorism titled, *"Who is ever alone?"* Nietzsche connects solitude with courage, saying, "The timid man does not know what it is to be alone: an enemy is always standing behind his chair. – Oh, if there were someone who could tell us the history of that subtle emotion called solitude!" And in D 382, Nietzsche says, "Out of damp and gloomy days, out of solitude, out of loveless words directed at us, *conclusions* grow up in us like fungus." It might seem that such morose thoughts would not be the deliverance of a virtue, but recall that, for Nietzsche, curious inquiry demands that the agent recognize and embrace all of reality – from the most ennobling to the most nauseating. In D 440, Nietzsche makes it clear that solitude helps in this endeavor: "To forego the world without knowing it, like a *nun* – that leads to a fruitless, perhaps melancholy solitude. It has nothing in common with the solitude of the *vita contemplativa* of the thinker: when he chooses *that* he is renouncing nothing." The thinker forgoes the *vita practica* "because he knows himself. Thus he leaps into *his* element, thus he gains *his* cheerfulness." In the next section, Nietzsche elaborates on this theme. The sort of solitude he favors is not empty, innocent, and ignorant. It is the solitude of someone who needs a little peace and quiet in order to attend to aspects of the human condition that are not immediately present. Thus, "The more we think about all that has been and will be, the paler grows that which is. If we live with the dead and die with them in their death, what are our 'neighbors' to us then? We grow more solitary – and we do so *because* the whole flood of humanity is surging around us." Such solitude is not for everyone. Like the other Nietzschean virtues, it belongs properly to Nietzsche and those who share his type. Moreover, even they may fail to develop and embody it for lack of education. In D 443, Nietzsche claims that "the most universal deficiency in our kind of cultivation and education" is that "no one learns, no one strives after, no one teaches – *the endurance of solitude*." Contemplating past, present, future, and merely possible exemplars is a task best carried out in solitude.

In D 453, Nietzsche suggests that he sees this task as a prelude to "construct-[ing] anew the laws of life and action" as replacements for Procrustean folk moralism, but he worries that "for this task our sciences of physiology, medicine, sociology, and solitude are not yet sufficiently sure of themselves: and it is from them that the foundation-stones of new ideals (if not the new ideals themselves) must come." In BGE 186, Nietzsche echoes this idea, arguing that in order to envision and embrace new values, we need first to survey, taxonomize, analyze, and empathize with "the tremendous realm of tender value feelings and value distinctions that live, grow, reproduce, and are destroyed," then construct a "*typology* of morals" that would serve as a kind of menu from which to select bespoke sets of values for the present and the future. Nietzsche thinks that solitude is a necessary virtue in this context because it helps one both to appreciate the positive values of cultures and societies that are (in multiple senses) foreign and to understand the serious flaws and shortcomings in one's own community.

In D 473 and D 481, Nietzsche returns to the idea that solitude is a virtue only for a particular type of person. In the former, he remarks, "If you feel yourself great and fruitful in solitude, a life in society will diminish you and make you empty: and *vice versa*." This idea is echoed in GS 359, where Nietzsche says that "solitude becomes poison in persons who have turned out badly." And in D 481, he says that Kant "has not experienced very much [. . . .] I am thinking, of course, not of crude 'events' impinging from without, but of the vicissitudes and convulsions which befall the most solitary and quietest life which possesses leisure and burns with the passion of thinking." This may be unfair to Kant, but the general point stands: only those with the curious intensity to make something of their solitude are likely to benefit from it. Such people have enough endogenously-arising thoughts and reflections to fuel their minds, whereas others would be barren and bored if they were not to be filled up by the thoughts of their neighbors. In D 491, Nietzsche stages a brief dialogue in which one of the characters says, "I go into solitude" to avoid taking from others. What is he afraid of taking? "When I am among the many I live as the many do, and I do not think as I really think." He's afraid of taking their thoughts, of adopting their values as a lazy default. In solitude, these are less salient, and he is able to think in his own way and direct his concerns as befits his own instincts and other drives.

In D 499, Nietzsche explores the social dynamics of this kind of solitude, saying that it is "a fact that, in the midst of society and sociability every evil inclination has to place itself under such great restraint, don so many masks, lay itself so often on the Procrustean bed of virtue, that one could well speak of a martyrdom of the evil man." By contrast, "In solitude all this falls away. He who is evil is at his most evil in solitude: which is where he is also at his best." Solitude draws out the more idiosyncratic and type-specific drives of the individual. It enhances individuality and authenticity. This does not mean that it necessarily fosters traditional and orthodox virtues. Rather, solitude incubates whatever drives are already present.

Turning next to *The Gay Science*, we find Nietzsche again pointing out that solitude is a psychological rather than a physical state. In GS 2, he declaims, "*the great majority lacks an intellectual conscience* – indeed, it has often seemed to me as if someone requiring such a conscience would be as solitary in the most densely populated cities as he would be in the desert." He then clarifies what he means by an intellectual conscience and its lack, saying, "*to the great majority* it is not contemptible to believe this or that and to live accordingly *without* first becoming aware of the final and most certain reasons pro and con, and without even troubling themselves about such reasons after." To have an intellectual conscience is thus a matter of refusing to accept the default beliefs, values, and way of life in one's community, but instead to engage one's curiosity to ask what reasons there are to accept or reject these beliefs and values. Nietzsche goes on to ask rhetorically, "what are goodheartedness, refinement, and genius to me when the person possessing these virtues tolerates slack feelings in his believing and judging and when he does not consider *the desire for certainty* to be his inmost craving and deepest need!"

Later, in GS 10, Nietzsche warns that if one embodies instincts and powers that are unusual in one's own community, one risks the "danger of becoming mad and lonely." In GS 35, he explicates this concern in terms of having drives that systematically position one in contravention of one's community: "To think otherwise than is customary is much less the effect of a superior intellect than of strong, evil drives – detaching, isolating, defiant, gloating, and malicious drives." He then goes on to say that "Heretics and witches are two species of evil people; what they have in common is that they also feel evil but are impelled by an unconquerable lust to harm what is prevailing (people or opinions)."

Solitude, from this point of view, is both a virtue and a danger to its bearer. This places it side by side with the other Nietzschean virtues. It's the sort of drive that, in the right person with the right set of other instincts and other drives, can lead to great and unusual accomplishments. But it's also liable to go wrong in other psychological or social contexts. In GS 50, Nietzsche pits solitude against the herd instinct:

> The reproach of conscience is weak in even the most conscientious people compared to the feeling: 'This or that is against the morals of *your* society.' Even the strongest person still *fears* a cold look or a sneer on the face of those among whom and for whom he has been brought up. What is he really afraid of? Growing solitude!

Nietzsche makes the same point in GS 117. Solitude verges, psychologically, on banishment. Only in those with the capacity to enjoy their solitude, those with a drive to – as Nietzsche puts it in HH "Pref" 1 – "unconditional *disparity of view*" are positioned to benefit from it. This is why true solitude, without even God or gods as witness, is the "invention" of "us, the godless" (GS 367).

The final passages of the first edition of the *Gay Science* are GS 341 and 342. In the former, Nietzsche introduces the idea of the eternal recurrence, which he frames in the context of "your most solitary solitude." In the latter, he introduces the figure of Zarathustra who, Nietzsche tells us, at the age of thirty "went into the mountains. There he enjoyed his spirit and solitude." This trope is repeated in the preface of *Thus Spoke Zarathustra* (Z "Pref" 1), and Zarathustra himself continually encounters solitude. For instance, in Z I "Tree," an unnamed youth says to Zarathustra, "If I am at the top then I always find myself alone. No one speaks with me, the frost of solitude makes me shiver." In Z I "Flies," Zarathustra urges his interlocutors, "Flee, my friend, into your solitude!" away from the flies of the marketplace. In Z III "Homecoming," Zarathustra returns to his solitude, saying, "Oh solitude! Oh you my *home* solitude!" The personified voice of solitude responds, saying, "Being forsaken is one thing, solitude another: *that* – you have now learned. And that among human beings you will always be wild and foreign." Thus we see again the distinction between the virtue of solitude, which Zarathustra here welcomes, and the pains of being forsaken or banished, which he deplores. Finally, in Z IV "Higher" 13, Nietzsche again indicates that solitude is a virtue only for those who embody a particular range of instincts, drives, and virtues; he puts the following words in Zarathustra's mouth: "Whatever one brings into solitude grows in it, even the inner beast. On this score, solitude is ill-advised for many." Solitude is thus the incubator of other drives and potentially a contributor to agentic integration.

Consider next *Beyond Good and Evil*. In BGE 25, Nietzsche recommends to the free spirits that they focus on asking questions rather than insisting on answers, and that they choose "the *good* solitude, the free, high-spirited, light-hearted solitude that, in some sense, gives you the right to stay good yourself!" In BGE 44, Nietzsche contrasts the type of the free spirit with the type of the free thinker, which represents "people without solitude." According to Nietzsche, the free spirits, unlike the free thinkers, are "At home in many countries of the spirit, at least as guests; repeatedly slipping away from the musty, comfortable corners where preference, prejudice, youth, origin, accidents of people, and books, and even the fatigue of traveling seem to have driven us." Once again, we see Nietzsche associate solitude with a sort of disagreeable drive, a disposition to get away from one's default community and their default beliefs, values, and way of life. He goes on to say that "we" free spirits embody various other virtues, such as curiosity and courage, and "are born, sworn, jealous friends of *solitude*, our own deepest, most midnightly, noon-lightly solitude. This is the type of people we are, we free spirits!" In a later passage (BGE 212), Nietzsche points to an important philosophical precedent for his sort of solitude: Socrates. The philosopher, he claims, "being *necessarily* a person of tomorrow and the day after tomorrow, has, in every age, been and has *needed* to be at odds with his today: his enemy has always been the ideal of today." Philosophers tend to feel like "disagreeable fools and dangerous question-marks." They are "the bad conscience of their age. In applying a vivisecting knife directly to the chest of the *virtues of the age*, they gave away their own secret: to know a *new* greatness in humanity, a new, untraveled path to human greatness." These philosophers show "how many lies are hidden beneath the most highly honored type of their present-day morality, and how much virtue is *out of date*." Nietzsche goes on to mention the figure of Socrates as an exemplar of this contrarian posture. In his own time, Nietzsche thinks, this contrarian impulse leads to the valorization of a specific form of life: "Greatest of all is the one who can be the most solitary, the most hidden, the most different, the person beyond good and evil, the master of his virtues."

This person or character is, of course, Zarathustra. In GM II:24, Nietzsche returns to Zarathustra, calling him "the *redeeming* man of great love and contempt, the creative spirit whose compelling strength will not let him rest in any aloofness or any beyond, whose solitude is misunderstood by the people as if it were flight *from* reality." Even Zarathustra, though, needs to alternate between love and contempt, between closeness and distance, between companionship and solitude. In GM III:14, Nietzsche says that those of higher types must not become the "physicians, consolers, and 'saviors' of the sick." Instead, he says, these higher types need "fresh air" and "good company, *our* company! Or solitude, if it must be!" This solitude guards against the "*great disgust at man! against great pity for man!*"

Turning finally to Nietzsche's late works, we again find the virtue of solitude and its relation to the other Nietzschean virtues. In the preface to *The Antichrist*, he says that "The conditions required to understand me" include honesty, being "used to living on mountains," having the "strength" for "questions that require more courage than anyone possesses today; a courage for the *forbidden*," and an "experience from out of seven solitudes."

A few passages from *Ecce Homo* provide the last bit of elucidation. In EH "Pref" 3, Nietzsche associates solitude with the pathos of distance, curiosity, and intellectual courage. In this passage, Nietzsche emphasizes that solitude is a virtue only for those who embody the corresponding type. You need, as he says, "to be made for it." But for those who enjoy these interlocking, idiosyncratic drives, solitude makes it possible to partake of *nitimur in vetitum* [striving for the forbidden]. The mutuality among the Nietzschean virtues also appears in EH "Wise" 8; after bragging about the sensitivity of his sense of disgust, Nietzsche declares, "my humanity is *not* consist in sympathizing with people as they are, but instead in *putting up with* the fact that I sympathize with them . . . My humanity is a constant self-overcoming." In this passage, Nietzsche recognizes the difficulty posed by these emotions; he claims that, to cope with them, "I need *solitude*, by which I mean recovery, a return to myself, the breath of a free, light, playful air." In EH "Clever" 10, he doubles down on the value of solitude, saying that "The slightest compulsion, a gloomy look, any sort of harsh tone in the throat, all these are objections to a person and even more to his work . . . You cannot have any nerves . . . Even *suffering* from solitude is an objection, – I have only ever suffered from multitudes."

Intellectual Courage

Nietzsche frequently celebrates courage, and he usually has intellectual courage in mind when he does so, as many commentators have pointed out. Although White (2001) does not address courage directly, he does discuss how Nietzschean honesty involves confronting and accepting epistemic threats, such as hard-to-bear insights. Harper (2015, p. 373), in a paper about honesty as "Nietzsche's thumbscrew," argues that, for Nietzsche, honesty is primarily a matter of being honest with *oneself.* As he says, "Nietzsche does acknowledge the importance of treating others, such as friends, with honesty. More commonly, though, Nietzsche's honesty is self-directed." Such self-directed honesty requires the courage to look reality in the eye, to see things as they really are, no matter how ugly, repulsive, or nauseating. In addition, Harper (2015, p. 374) characterizes honesty as a drive. As such, it is best understood not in terms of states like knowledge and belief but in terms of the active process of inquiry. "Nietzsche presents honesty as an activity rather than a state, as it is something continually employed and 'perfected'." Harper also convincingly argues that Nietzschean truthfulness always involves confrontation, which may be social (e.g., telling people what they don't want to hear) but is more typically epistemic (e.g., asking hard questions and embracing the answers even when the truth is terrible). Third, Jenkins (2016) also approaches the virtue of courage via truthfulness about facts that are hard to accept and even harder to embrace, saying that the will to truth is "closely tied to the virtue of courage" and that the "maximally truthful person [. . .] is always disposed to sacrifice other things she values in order to be in touch with the truth." What distinguishes truthfulness, on this view, from other dispositions and virtues is "the remarkable *difficulty* of pursuing the truth." Finally, Kuehne (2018) emphasizes Nietzsche's frequent discussions of the moral and intellectual dangers posed by "complacent thinking and entrenched belief systems disintegrating." According to Kuehne, responding adequately to these dangers requires one to "live courageously," which he glosses in terms of "identifying the paradoxes that beset our knowledge and moral beliefs." Each of these commentators attributes to Nietzsche a position consistent with the portrait of courage that I paint here. However, they approach courage only obliquely, via truthfulness, honesty, or danger.

In *Human, All-Too-Human*, Nietzsche has a lot to say about courage. For example, in HH 134 he describes courage in affective terms, suggesting that courageous action is motivated by characteristic feelings and moods. In HH 164, which addresses the nature and frequent misapprehension of genius, Nietzsche says that the "purely human qualities" characteristic of genius include "undiminishing energy, resolute application to individual goals, great personal courage, [. . .] good fortune to receive an upbringing which offered in the early years the finest teachers, models, and methods." Here, we see Nietzsche associate courage not with facing down physical or martial dangers but with the intellectual pursuits of the genius. HH 308 is a one-sentence aphorism: "One can persuade courageous people to participate in an action by representing it as being more dangerous than it is." In the *Assorted Opinions and Maxims,* Nietzsche offers further thoughts about courage. In HH AOM 177 Nietzsche praises "the ladder, the courage, and the skill" of artists who "dare" to represent "the highest forms of moral perfection." When Nietzsche talks about courage, the exemplars he has in mind are typically not soldiers, generals, or bushwhackers. They are geniuses, artists, and other adventurers in the intellectual domain.

Turning next to *Daybreak*, in D 146, Nietzsche contrasts a sort of local and temporally proximal other-regarding consequentialism with "a higher and freer viewpoint," which enjoins us to "*look beyond* these immediate consequences to others and under certain circumstances to pursue more distant goals *even at the cost of the suffering of others.*" While this criticism betrays a misunderstanding of consequentialism as a normative doctrine, it does stand as a critique of folk morality, which tends to focus myopically on proximal causes and effects. What sorts of suffering in others does Nietzsche envisage? He thinks that it may be virtuous "to pursue knowledge even though one realizes that our free-spiritedness will at first and as an immediate consequence plunge others into doubt, grief, and even worse things." These are the sorts of harms and dangers that would be best faced by someone possessed of intellectual courage. And indeed, Nietzsche goes on to say that he and those who share his type face and overcome the same intellectual challenges that might crush others.

In D 154, Nietzsche makes it clear that the sort of intellectual courage he considers a virtue in his own type would be unrecognizable in other types of people and other social contexts. He contrasts the ancient Greeks, for whom "great perils and upheavals were always present," with his comfortable contemporaries. The former "sought in knowledge and reflection a kind of security and ultimate *refugium*. We, in our incomparably more secure condition, have transferred this recklessness into knowledge and reflection." As a drive, this recklessness preexists any dangers and threats it may eventually oppose. In the one case (the Greeks), this results in martial courage. In the other (in Nietzsche's type and time), in intellectual courage. He returns to this theme in D 501, where he argues that one benefit of atheism is that it does not force people to try to achieve absolute certainty about difficult questions on pain of eternal damnation. In overcoming theism, he says, we have "reconquered our courage for error, for experimentation, for accepting provisionally." This courage for error is opposed to the theological need for certainty that Nietzsche elsewhere calls an "*intellectual vice*" (D 543) and allied instead with the virtues of curiosity and solitude, thus contributing to agentic integration.

But such enjoyment in experimentation and fallibilistic inquiry is not for everyone. In an aphorism titled *"Courage to suffer"* (D 354), Nietzsche contends that "we are able to endure a fairly large amount of unpleasure, and our stomach is designed to take this heavy fare. Perhaps without it we would find life's repast insipid: and without our ready tolerance of pain we should have to give up too many pleasures!" Nietzsche also compares learning to eating in GS 110, where he asks, "To what extent can truth endure incorporation?" The metaphor is especially apt given his drive psychology. Just as hunger is a drive that impels one characteristic form of activity (eating) and evaluation (seeing food as desirable), so intellectual courage is a drive that impels its own characteristic form of activity (inquiry) and evaluation (appreciation of uncertainty and the opportunity to ask and answer questions). Courage here supports the agent's curiosity, thereby contributing to agentic integration.

Next, in D 395, Nietzsche addresses the emotional context of philosophizing. "With one thinker," he tells us, "the reflective state peculiar to the thinker always succeeds a state of fear, with another it always succeeds a state of desire." Different types of thinkers demonstrate characteristically different affective patterns in their inquiries. For those who tend to reach their conclusions after overcoming fear, "reflectiveness seems to be associated with a feeling of *security*" and a "happy and courageous mood." They might even acquire a taste for dangerous inquiries. This is what happens to the unnamed character in the dialogue Nietzsche stages in D 477, who declares, "Others emerge out of a general moral skepticism ill-humored and feeble, gnawed-at and worm-eaten, indeed half-consumed – but I do so more courageous and healthier than ever, again in possession of my instincts." In this passage, courage is portrayed as contributing to both emotional integrity and agentic integration.

The Gay Science offers further material to illuminate Nietzsche's conception of courage. In GS "Pref" 2, he says that he is waiting for a "philosophical *physician*" to "summon the courage at last to push my suspicion to its limit." He then says that courageously pushing suspicion to the limit entails arguing that "what was at stake in all philosophizing hitherto was not at all 'truth' but rather something else – let us say health, future, growth, power, life." The courage in question here is clearly intellectual and emotional. It's the courage to doubt common opinion, to approach received wisdom with suspicion. As such, this courage supports solitude and agentic integration.

Later, in GS 39, Nietzsche makes it clear that he thinks intellectual courage is grounded in embodied processes. He praises exemplars of strong taste who "have the courage to own up to their *physis* and to heed its demands down to its subtlest tones." Once again, courage is associated with the intellectual rather than the martial domain. It's the sort of thing that enables someone to be true to themselves. Next, in GS 388, Nietzsche returns to the problem of the subtlest tones of psychic economy. In this passage, he recommends helping "only those whose distress you properly *understand* because they share with you one suffering and one hope – your *friends* – and only in the way you help yourself." Nietzsche suggests that it would be futile, counterproductive, or perhaps just uncouth to offer help when one does not understand the predicament and type of the person helped. He also recommends a revision of the golden rule: not *do unto others as you would have them do unto you* but *do unto others as you would do unto yourself*. What, in this context, would Nietzsche do to help himself to cope with his own idiosyncratic suffering? He answers, "I want to make them more courageous, more persevering, simpler, more full of gaiety." As I already pointed out, Nietzschean courage is not for everyone. In this passage, he commends it only to himself and his friends, those who share his psychological type. In GS 373, likewise, Nietzsche declares that it follows "from the laws that govern rank-ordering that scholars, insofar as they belong to the intellectual middle class, are not even allowed to catch sight of the truly *great* problems and question marks; moreover, their courage and eyes simply don't reach that far." The implication is that those who do not belong to the right type simply cannot appreciate, let alone answer, the questions that excite Nietzsche and those of his type. The Nietzschean virtues are quixotic. Moreover, he suggests that even if they could approach these questions, they lack the intellectual courage to take them on. One must embody the right drives to engage in this kind of inquiry. One must have a soul that "thirsts to experience the whole range of previous values and aspirations" and be "more courageous, perhaps, than is prudent" (GS 382).

Turn now to *Beyond Good and Evil*. In BGE 5, Nietzsche contrasts the "courage of conscience" characteristic of someone who attains and expresses self-knowledge even about shameful truths with wishful thinking. Courage of conscience here involves a willingness both to know oneself and to speak that knowledge to others. Next, in BGE 30, Nietzsche again claims that the questions and answers that attract someone of his type must remain opaque to those who embody a different type: "Our highest insights must – and should! – sound like stupidities, or possibly crimes, when they come without permission to people whose ears are not of our type." Once again, we see that the kind of courage Nietzsche prizes in his own type is a form of intellectual courage, and that it is not recommended as a universal Procrustean virtue but only as a type-relative virtue.

For the philosophical type, though, this sort of questioning is entirely appropriate. Nietzsche goes so far as to claim that the philosopher "has a *duty* to suspicion today, to squint maliciously out of every abyss of suspicion" (BGE 34). The skepticism evinced here aims to disconfirm cherished notions about human nature. Thus, the epistemic emotion of mistrust is closely tied to the Nietzschean intellectual virtues. People are typically motivated to search for counterexamples to claims when they're skeptical about those claims. From this point of view, skepticism is a spur to inquiry, a tool to be deployed by someone who wants to inquire well. Nietzsche describes a range of further allied dispositions in BGE 45, where he catalogs the qualities needed by someone who shares his own peculiar inquisitiveness as "courage, intelligence, and subtlety." When these drives enjoy agentic and evaluative integration, they are type-relative virtues. While there is no guarantee that someone will manage to achieve such integration, Nietzsche celebrates the lucky cases and moments when "we gather the courage to reconceive our evils as what is best in us" (BGE 116).

Later, in BGE 209, Nietzsche claims that a single trait ("virile skepticism") expresses itself as various intellectual virtues: "now, for example, as an intrepid eye, now as the courage and hardness of analysis, as the tough will to undertake dangerous journeys of exploration and spiritualized North Pole expeditions." And in BGE 227, Nietzsche recommends that we "dispatch to [our honesty's] assistance whatever we have in us of devilry: our disgust with what is clumsy and approximate, our '*nitimur in vetitum*' [we strive for the forbidden], our adventurous courage, our seasoned and choosy curiosity." Finally, in BGE 284, Nietzsche lists four essential virtues: "courage, insight, sympathy, and solitude."

At the same time that he was assembling *Beyond Good and Evil*, Nietzsche wrote the new prefaces for *Human, All-Too-Human* and *The Birth of Tragedy*. The former contains a motherlode of engagement with courage. In HH "Pref" 1, he declares, "My writings have been called a schooling in suspicion, even more in contempt, but fortunately also in courage." The courage he has in mind is intellectual. It's a drive that gives one the aplomb to question where others shrink away. Nietzsche goes on to remind us that he is of the devil's party: "I myself do not believe that anyone has ever before looked into the world with an equally profound degree of suspicion, and not merely as an occasional devil's advocate, but, to speak theologically, just as much as an enemy and indicter of God." Nietzsche brags of his intellectual courage, which impels him to inquire suspiciously about sacred cows and sacred values. This requires courage both because it may reveal unpleasant truths about oneself and because it positions one in opposition to one's community. Nietzsche describes such opposition in terms of the "fears and frosts of the solitude" to which "unconditional *disparity of view* condemns him who is infected with it."

The preface added to the *Assorted Opinions and Maxims* also celebrates intellectual courage. In HH AOM "Pref" 6, Nietzsche commends his books "to *you*, who have the hardest fate, you rare, most imperiled, most spiritual, most courageous men who have to be the *conscience* of the modern soul and as such have to possess its *knowledge*, and in whom all that exists today of sickness, poison, and danger comes together." As a reward, Nietzsche says, his chosen readers will be granted knowledge of "the way to a *new* health." Note that Nietzsche does not recommend intellectual courage to just anyone. Rather, he suggests that it is a virtue only for a very specific type of person, the "rare, most imperiled, most spiritual." But in this type, intellectual courage is allied with the person's other drives. As such, they are able to ask the questions and embrace the answers before which others would falter. In the next section (HH AOM "Pref" 7), Nietzsche contrasts romantic pessimism with "a will to the tragic and to pessimism that is as much a sign of severity and strength of intellect (taste, feeling, conscience)." This latter sort of pessimism is a drive that motivates intellectually courageous inquiry. "With this will in one's heart one has no fear of the fearful and questionable that characterizes all existence; one even seeks it out. Behind such a will there stands courage, pride, the longing for a *great* enemy. – This has been *my* pessimistic perspective from the beginning." This "longing" for an enemy is typical of Nietzschean drives, which impel characteristic forms of activity and evaluation. Someone who embodies the Nietzschean form of intellectual courage is spoiling for an intellectual fight; the only question is where his courage will be expressed, not whether it will be expressed.

Nietzsche also provides food for thought about courage in the *Genealogy*. For example, in GM I:1, while speaking of the "English psychologists," he expresses the hope that they "may be fundamentally courageous, proud, and magnanimous animals, who [. . .] have trained themselves to sacrifice all desirability to truth, *every* truth, even plain, harsh, ugly, repellent, unchristian, immoral truth. – For such truths do exist." Courage here is associated with self-examination and criticism of one's community. It enables one to maintain composure and avoid wishful thinking while inquiring into the terrible truths. Nietzsche returns to this theme in GM I:14, where he asks who "has the courage" to "take a look into the secret of how *ideals are made* on earth," then ushers his reader, "Mr. Rash and Curious" into the "dark workshop." Three times, the narrator of this work is so overcome with nausea that he screams, "Enough! Enough!" (GM I:14, 2.25, and 3.27). The "subterranean" adventure of *Genealogy* is "painful" (GM II:6); it's at once "interesting" and full of "a gloomy, black, unnerving sadness" (GM II:22). The inquisitor wants to believe the truth because he wants to overcome the resistance that interesting, hard problems afford.

This attraction to challenging inquiry also crops up in GM III:9, where Nietzsche argues that the drives characteristic of the philosophical type make them "the embodiment of '*nitimur in vetitum*'." The Latin phrase, which Nietzsche also uses in BGE 227 and EH "Pref" 3, is from Ovid's *Amores* Book 3. It's a quotation from the fourth elegy on adultery, in which Ovid recommends against strict enforcement of the norm of chastity. *Nitimur in vetitum* – we strive for the forbidden – expresses the idea that something becomes more attractive to the extent that getting it is challenging. Whereas in Ovid's case the forbidden fruit is adulterous sex, in Nietzsche's case, it is the fruit of the tree of the knowledge of good and evil. Philosophers, whom he is here ironically characterizing as adherents to the *ascetic* ideal, are just like adulterous spouses. Their drives impel them toward precisely what they're not allowed to have. Whereas in the adulterer's case the drive in question is the sex drive, in the philosophers' case, a whole host of epistemic drives are in play: His drive to doubt, his drive to deny, his drive to suspend judgment (his 'ephectic' drive), his drive to analyze, his drive to investigate, seek, dare, his drive to compare and balance, his will to neutrality and objectivity, his will to every '*sine ira et studio*'.

In the philosophical type, these drives are candidates for being virtues to the extent that they enjoy agentic and evaluative integration. It's obvious that the drives just listed could enjoy agentic integration. Nietzsche argues that they may not so easily enjoy evaluative integration because they contravene "the basic demands of morality and conscience." For this reason, he says, the early philosopher strategically avoided expressing his intellectual courage and other epistemic drives in easily legible ways. In so doing, he both saved himself from inviting intense social disapprobation and kept a clear conscience. He "*guarded* against 'feeling himself,' against becoming conscious of himself'" in order to preserve his feeling of integrity.

The late works demonstrate Nietzsche's continued interest in intellectual courage. For example, in the preface to *The Antichrist*, he spells out what he takes to be the "conditions required to understand me." The virtues he lists include being "honest to the point of hardness," "used to living on mountains," "indifferent" to the suffering caused by inquiry, never asking "whether truth does any good, whether it will be our undoing," a "drive" to ask "questions that require more courage than anyone possesses today; a courage for the *forbidden*," an "experience from out of seven solitudes." These traits run contrary to the instincts and other drives that Nietzsche associates with Christianity. In A 21, he tells us, "It is Christian to hate *spirit*, to hate pride, courage, freedom, libertinism of the spirit." In A 46 he declares that "there is nothing free, kind, candid, or honest" about the New Testament. "There are only *bad* instincts in the New Testament, there is not even the courage for those bad instincts. Everything is cowardice, everything is closed-eyes and self-deceit."

Turning next to *Twilight of the Idols*, in TI "Arrows" 2 Nietzsche again demonstrates that, when he talks about courage, he means intellectual courage: "Even the most courageous among us only rarely has courage for what he really *knows*." In TI "Socrates" 11, he speculates that Socrates may, "in the *wisdom* of his death-bed courage" have displayed such intellectual courage when it came to knowledge of the Nietzschean conception of happiness ("happiness is equal to instinct"). This is a difficult truth to stomach, let alone embrace. But, in Nietzsche's view, Socrates had high spirits and the "most spiritual people (assuming they are the most courageous) experience by far the most painful tragedies: but this is precisely why they honor life, because it provides them with their greatest adversities" (TI "Skirmishes" 17).

One exemplar of this sort of courage is Thucydides (TI "Ancients" 2). In this passage, Nietzsche praises Thucydides, saying, "Thucydides, and perhaps Machiavelli's *Principe*, are most closely related to me in terms of their unconditional will not to be fooled and to see reason in *reality*." He goes on to celebrate "Thucydides as the great summation, the final manifestation of that strong, severe, harsh objectivity that lay in the instincts of the more ancient Hellenes. In the end, what divides natures like Thucydides from natures like Plato is *courage* in the face of reality." In Thucydides's case, intellectual courage was an instinct; in other cases it might be an acquired drive. Either way, it's a virtue in those who share Thucydides's type.

Finally, in *Ecce Homo* Nietzsche returns to the theme of *nitimur in vetitum*, saying, "my philosophy will triumph under this sign, because it is precisely the truth that has been absolutely forbidden so far" (EH "Pref" 3). What does he have in mind when he refers to "my philosophy" in this section? Not any specific doctrine, argument, proposition, or axiom, but a set of virtues. As before, the virtues commended in this section are not for everyone. They are to some extent instinctual, the sort of thing one can be "made for." He goes on to say, "How much truth can a spirit *tolerate*, how much truth is it willing to *risk*? This increasingly became the real measure of value for me." The process of confronting, incorporating, accepting, and embracing terrible truths *is* Nietzsche's philosophy. This is what he means when he praises the virtues of curiosity, solitude, and courage. From this vantage point, error "is not blindness, error is *cowardice* ... Every achievement, every step forward in knowledge, comes from *courage*." In EH "Books" 3, Nietzsche returns to these same allied virtues (for those, and only those, who can manage them), saying of his own books that "they sometimes reach the highest elevation you will find anywhere on earth, cynicism; you need the most delicate fingers as well as the most courageous fists to conquer them." Of *Thus Spoke Zarathustra,* in particular he says that, to understand it, "you need to have *harshness* in your habits, if you are going to be cheerful among harsh truths. When I imagine a perfect reader, I always think of a monster of courage and curiosity who is also supple, cunning, cautious, a born adventurer and discoverer." In EH "Books" BGE 2 Nietzsche adds solitude to the list of virtues fitting for his own type. Here he says of *Beyond Good and Evil* that it is "in essence a *critique of modernity*," and that "You need courage in your body in order just to stand it, you need to never have learned fear ... All the things this age is proud of are viewed as conflicting with [a higher psychological] type."

Having a Sense of Humor

Nietzsche, in addition to sometimes being uproariously funny, reflects more on laughter than almost any other philosopher. Several scholars have further noticed that Nietzschean laughter sometimes seems to have an epistemic function. Jason Wirth (2005) argues on the basis of *Thus Spoke Zarathustra* that Nietzsche uses laughter to affirm philosophical truths. Lawrence Hatab (1988) likewise characterizes Nietzschean laughter as an affirmative response to terrible truths. Mark Weeks (2004) argues that, while Nietzsche does sometimes use laughter to affirm, he remains ambivalent about the role of laughter in philosophy. Mordechai Gordon (2016) says that Nietzsche imagines humor and laughter as ways to confront the problem of nihilism. Keith Ansell-Pearson (1994, p. 102) argues that the political stance of Zarathustra in the face of nihilism must be that of a parodist. Drawing on Morreall's (1983, p. 123) analysis of a humorous attitude toward life in terms of distance from life's practical aspects, Lippitt (1992, p. 45) contends that, at the end of book 3, Zarathustra is able to laugh at himself and the type of person he represents, thus demonstrating such an attitude by exhibiting "flexibility and openness to experience." Zarathustra recommends reflexive laughter to the wrecks of the higher men in Z "Higher" 15 and calls himself "Zarathustra the soothsayer [*Wahrsager*], Zarathustra the soothlaugher [*Wahrlacher*]" in Z IV "Higher" 18. Nicholas More (2014) argues in *Nietzsche's Last Laugh* that *Ecce Homo* should be read not as a bizarre and self-congratulatory autobiography but as philosophical satire. Kathleen Higgins (2000) devotes a book-length interpretation of *The Gay Science* to accounting for Nietzsche's humor, arguing that he uses it to engage his readers' imaginative capacities. In an earlier article, Higgins (1994) contends that Nietzsche employs laughter in *The Genealogy of Morals* to shock his readers out of their complacent attitudes, resulting in the realization that much that they'd held dear was nonsense. In his treatment of Nietzsche's "gags" in *Beyond Good and Evil*, Nickolas Pappas (2005) distinguishes the laughter of a community at those it excludes (moralizing and ostracizing laughter) from the laughter that a solitary individual directs back at a community she finds ridiculous and whose contempt she welcomes (what Nietzsche refers to as *spernere se sperni*). According to Pappas, solitary laughter of this sort can only find its echo in an imagined future audience for whom moral concepts and words are playthings that can be bandied about in a detached or ironic mode. Finally, Ansell-Pearson & Serini (2022) point out that humor and intellectual courage are frequently aligned in Nietzsche's thinking.

Thus, nearly a dozen commentators have remarked on Nietzsche's laughter and use of humor. However, they have generally restricted their commentary to moments of laughter or episodes of humor. Few have addressed the topic of the *sense of* humor as a disposition of an agent, especially one that might constitute a virtue. Could having a sense of humor be a virtue? And, if it is, how should we characterize that virtue? In BGE 25, Nietzsche complains about philosophers who respond to terrible truths with "moral indignation," saying that this is "the unfailing sign in a philosopher that his philosophical sense of humor has left him." Later, in BGE 294, he goes further, saying, "I should actually risk an order of rank among philosophers depending on the rank of their laughter – all the way up to those capable of *golden* laughter. And supposing that gods, too, philosophize," he continues, "I should not doubt that they also know how to laugh the while in a superhuman and new way – and at the expense of all serious things. Gods enjoy mockery: it seems they cannot suppress laughter even during holy rites."

I contend that Nietzsche primarily uses humor and laughter for epistemic purposes. His epistemic aims include enabling inquiry that leads to the affirmation of hard truths, enabling inquiry that leads to negation of cherished illusions, and connecting with other inquirers who belong to the same psychological type. A sense of humor supports these goals by inducing contempt and the laughter that expresses (and sometimes also conjures) it.

For Nietzsche, a sense of humor is essential to opening up the path to inquiry into the laughable and contemptible. Some of these inquiries terminate in laughing affirmation of truths that would be hard to take without a mirthful buffer. Others terminate in laughing negation of cherished illusions. And some of the most important inquiries that having a sense of humor fosters are into oneself, one's own character, and one's community. Nietzsche thinks that the ability to laugh at oneself – to play the role of both the producer and the object – makes possible both self-knowledge and self-overcoming. In Z IV "Higher" 15, Zarathustra enjoins the higher men: "Learn to laugh at yourselves as one must laugh!" And in BGE 191, Nietzsche asks of Socrates, "didn't he spend his whole life laughing at the shortcomings of his clumsy, noble Athenians, who, like all noble people, were men of instinct and could never really account for why they acted the way they did? But in the end, silently and secretly, he laughed at himself as well?" Someone who is able to laugh at their own imperfections is also, sometimes, able to see those imperfections as unimportant. This makes it possible to abandon them, to change, to become a different and perhaps more worthy and interesting person.

One might worry that laughter, because it expresses contempt and a judgment that something is unimportant, nonsensical, or unworthy, is in tension with the effective inquiry. Nietzsche thinks otherwise, as he says in GS 327: "And 'where laughter and gaiety are found, thinking is good for nothing' – that is the prejudice of this serious beast against all 'gay science'. Well then, let us prove it a prejudice!" A sense of humor fosters inquiry into truths that are hard to stomach. This is an essential first step in Nietzsche's curiosity-centered epistemology.

An enduring theme in Nietzsche's philosophy is that there are some truths that people find hard to consider, harder to accept, and even harder to embrace. These include unflattering truths of moral psychology. For many people, inquiring at all – let alone successfully – into such truths is opposed by tender feelings, veneration, and faith. Faith is "a *veto* on science" because it involves "not *wanting* to know the truth" (A 52). The faithful person prefers to terminate investigation. Compassion for hurt feelings – whether one's own or those of others – constrains inquiry into the hard truths that Nietzsche finds so fascinating (BT 3, GM I:1, EH "Destiny" 1, EH "Destiny" 5, TI "Reason" 6). In order to overcome this opposition, Nietzsche thinks, we sometimes need to laugh at our faith, the objects of our veneration, and our own tender feelings. This is why he says that, "In a man of knowledge, pity is almost laughable, like delicate hands on a cyclops" (BGE 171).

Accepting these hard truths without falling into nihilism also requires laughter. In section 7 of the "Attempt at Self-criticism" that Nietzsche appended to *The Birth of Tragedy*, he sheepishly admits that much of the book is nonsense, but he maintains a commitment to a kind of cheerful pessimism that, he says, forestalls nihilism. He goes on to recommend the same kind of cheerful pessimism to his audience and critics, telling them, "You should first learn the art of comfort *in this world*, you should learn to *laugh* my young friends, if you are really determined to remain pessimists." Such laughter inures the laugher against nihilism, which is one of the reasons why Nietzsche insists that his philosophy can be aptly described as gay science. Likewise, in BGE 62, Nietzsche claims that, "If you could survey the strangely painful, crude yet subtle comedy of European Christianity with the mocking and disinterested eye of an Epicurean god, I think you would find it to be a constant source of amazement and laughter." Such cheerful pessimism is possible for someone who adopts a divine perspective, looking down on themselves and indeed on two millennia of European history.

Just as a Nietzschean sense of humor can open up inquiries that terminate in the laughing acceptance of hard truths, so it can also lead to inquiries that terminate in the laughing negation of cherished illusions. Some laughter arises from adopting an affective and evaluative perspective from which the target of laughter is risible or contemptible. In particular, laughing together with a like-minded community at someone or something is liable to undermine any confidence the laughers had in the mindset and values associated with the target of their laughter. The target is liable to appear nonsensical or not worthy of being taken seriously.

In D 210, Nietzsche begins by distinguishing the question "what is laughable?" from "what is laughter?" He then goes on to claim that nothing is laughable in itself, "but there are states of soul in which we impose such words upon things external to and within us." Thus, the property of being ridiculous is imputed by ridiculing and laughing. And in D 291, Nietzsche defines presumptuousness as "the hypocritical pretense of incapacity for hypocrisy," which is so paradoxical that it almost always fails. He then suggests that, when someone fails to be presumptuous, "we laugh at him" because he has failed both to deceive us and to show himself superior to us.

These themes also crop up in *The Gay Science*. In GS 3, for example, Nietzsche claims that for "common natures all noble, magnanimous feelings appear to be inexpedient and therefore initially incredible: they give a wink when they hear of such things [. . .] they are suspicious of the noble person, as if he were furtively seeking his advantage." It's hard for common natures to accept that someone would be genuinely or sincerely magnanimous. However, "If they become all too clearly convinced of the absence of selfish intentions and gains, they view the noble person as a kind of fool: they despise him in his pleasure and laugh at the sparkle in his eye." Here we have an example of laughter that responds with ridicule to something that seems either nonsensical or out of step with the laugher's values. Nietzsche goes on: "The unreason or odd reason [*Unvernunft oder Quervernunft*] of passion is what the common type despises in the noble, especially when this passion is directed at objects whose value seems quite fantastic and arbitrary," such as "a passion for knowledge." Given that curiosity and intellectual courage are two of the chief virtues in the Nietzschean type, it should be clear that he envisions himself as precisely the sort of noble-minded person described in this passage. And in GS 346, he writes

> The whole attitude of 'man *against* the world', of man as a 'world-negating' principle, of man as the measure of the value of things, as judge of the world who finally places existence itself on his scales and finds it too light – the monstrous stupidity of this attitude has finally dawned on us and we are sick of it; we laugh as soon as we encounter the juxtaposition of 'man *and* world', separated by the sublime presumptuousness of the little word 'and'!

Nietzsche then goes on to suggest that such contemptuous laughter destroys veneration, and without anything to venerate one is liable to fall into nihilism. Laughter is thus both a cause of and a cure for nihilism. It enables people to give up their most cherished beliefs, which can lead to nihilism, but it also helps them maintain a positive affective orientation, which keeps nihilism at bay.

If this is right, then a sense of humor and the laughter it generates play an epistemic role in Nietzsche's philosophy: dislodging comfortable illusions that would otherwise be hard to examine and abandon. Even in the face of strong counter-evidence, people tend not to revise or abandon such beliefs and attitudes. Furthermore, when they do revise them, they tend to do so in irrational ways. This problem arises especially in connection with beliefs that are also imbued with emotion. Laughter that expresses contempt shakes loose affectively-tinged doxastic states that would otherwise be hard or impossible to revise, reject, or even review. As Zarathustra puts it, "Not by wrath does one kill, but by laughing" (Z I "Reading"). Likewise, in Z II "Tarantulas," Zarathustra says to the preachers of equality, "But I want to expose your hiding places to the light; therefore I laugh into your face my laughter of the heights." And in Z I "Teachers," Zarathustra "laughs inwardly" when he realizes that the teacher of virtue is a fool whose only insight is how to sleep well.

Next, in BGE 11, Nietzsche dismisses Kant's *Critique of Pure Reason* with incisive laughter: 'How are synthetic judgments *a priori* possible?' Kant asked himself – and what really is his answer? '*By virtue of a faculty*' – but unfortunately not in five words, but so circumstantially, venerably, and with such a display of German profundity and curlicues that people simply failed to note the laughable *niaiserie allemande* involved in such an answer.

Like most philosophers, Nietzsche offers reasons and arguments for his positions; unlike most other philosophers, he tries to cement his reasoning and argumentation rhetorically by inducing laughter at his targets. If these targets are seen as ridiculous and nonsensical, his audience is more likely to be moved. This is especially important when the target of laughter is oneself or some aspect of oneself. In GM III:3, Nietzsche claims that the "ultimate pinnacle" of artistic greatness is achieved when the artist "comes to see himself and his art *beneath him* – when he knows how to *laugh* at himself." The context is Wagner's late career. In this passage Nietzsche claims, perhaps a bit tongue-in-cheek, that "one might be tempted" to think that "the Wagnerian *Parsifal* was intended as a joke, as a kind of epilogue and satyr play with which the tragedian Wagner wanted to take leave of us, also of himself, above all *of tragedy* in a fitting manner worthy of himself, namely with an extravagance of wanton parody."

Nietzsche also discusses reflexive laughter in HH 137, a passage about self-defiance and self-overcoming. He argues that some people take "real delight in oppressing themselves with excessive claims and afterwards idolizing this tyrannically demanding something in their soul." Such self-overcoming leads to various seemingly foolhardy endeavors: "Thus a man climbs on dangerous paths in the highest mountains so as to laugh mockingly at his fears and trembling knees; thus a philosopher adheres to views of asceticism, humility, and holiness in the light of which his own image becomes extremely ugly." In the same vein, in GS 107 Nietzsche says, "At times we need to have a rest from ourselves by looking at and down at ourselves and, from an artistic distance, laughing *at* ourselves or crying *at* ourselves." He goes on, saying, "we have to discover the *hero* no less than the *fool* in our passion for knowledge; we must now and then be pleased about our folly in order to be able to stay pleased about our wisdom." And in GS 1, Nietzsche offers this somewhat perplexing challenge: "To laugh at oneself as one would have to laugh in order to laugh *from the whole truth* – for that, not even the best have had enough sense of truth, and the most gifted have had far too little genius!"

6 Conclusion

Nietzsche's immoralism has been the subject of debate for decades. Almost every possible metaethical position has been attributed to him, many of them inconsistent with attributing a positive, substantive virtue theory to him at the normative level. In this Element, I sidestepped the question of what meta-ethical position he adopts, in part because his relevant remarks can seem self-contradictory and in part because they do not easily map onto the taxonomy of views in contemporary anglophone metaethics where the interpretive debate has been conducted. Instead, I set out to show that, regardless of his metaethical views, he had a well-developed and idiosyncratic theory of virtue that ranges across moral and epistemic virtues.

This analysis was motivated and guided by the insights of the digital humanities methodology described briefly in the introduction and at greater length in Alfano (2019). That methodology revealed that Nietzsche grew more interested in virtue in his middle works, and that this interest was sustained through the late works. The concepts Nietzsche tends to discuss most frequently when talking about virtue are chastity, contempt, courage, cruelty, fear, honesty, justice, life, modesty, nobility, rank, shame, solitude, value, and vice. In subsequent sections, I constructed an account of Nietzschean virtue that engages closely with the passages in which he addresses these concepts.

I began laying the groundwork by explaining Nietzsche's conceptions of drives and instincts. These are the basic building blocks of his moral psychology (and also, as Riccardi 2021 has argued, his philosophical psychology more broadly). Instincts and other drives motivate both action and evaluation. In different contexts, the same drive will impel quite different actions – including, in some cases, actions that are detrimental to the agent. Different drives cluster together in populations. When such a cluster exists, Nietzsche calls it a type. Some types are very common, others rare or even unique to a single individual. Drives are relatively stable dispositions, though they are susceptible to cultural and individual modulation to some extent. This in turn means that types are also relatively stable.

I then turned to Nietzsche's normative views, arguing that, for him, virtues are a subset of drives. However, because people belong to different types, this means that the drives that are virtues for one person may be non-virtues or even vices in another person. A drive is a virtue for an individual only when it contributes to what Nietzsche variously calls life, health, and flourishing. Drives do so when they enjoy agentic integration and evaluative integration. Agentic integration occurs when the expression of one drive does not stymie the expression of another drive or, in stronger cases, when the expression of one drive is also the expression of another drive. Evaluative integration occurs when the expression of a drive does not lead to strong negative attitudes, such as guilt and shame, toward fixed aspects of the self, or in stronger cases, when the expression of the drive leads to positive self-evaluations such as pride and self-esteem. This means that Nietzsche holds a type-relative unity-of-virtue thesis, which is quite different from more familiar virtue theories derived from Plato and Aristotle among others. It sets him against what he sometimes calls Procrustean moralism, which dictates that whatever is a virtue for one must be a virtue for all. Nietzsche is thus a champion of human diversity who insists that psychological differences deserve recognition, and that the universalizing impulses of, for instance, Christianity do violence to many people's psychologies – undermining their agency and inducing unnecessary self-torment.

Because we are deeply social animals, our self-evaluations are strongly influenced by our communities. We learn values and norms from our communities in childhood and throughout our lives. We are also attuned to both the negative attitudes, such as resentment, contempt, and disgust, and the positive attitudes, such as admiration, gratitude, and respect, that others direct toward us. For this reason, evaluative integration is dependent on one's familial relationships, intimate relationships, friendships, collegial relations, and broader collective identities – not all of which are elective.

Nietzsche was not the first philosopher to notice that people care about what others think and feel about them. In fact, he argues that almost everyone is aware of this. For this reason, we sometimes express emotions toward others that function as self-fulfilling prophecies. When we show or tell people what we think of them, and their underlying drive structure answers to some extent to that description, they may end up adopting the ascription and behaving even more in accord with it. At the same time, we sometimes show or tell people what we think of ourselves; if they accept the self-ascription, that provides us with social proof that makes us more sure of our own self-concepts. These processes can be explicit and manipulative, but Nietzsche thinks that they can also be innocent and even ennobling.

In addition, the way our drives get expressed can be influenced by the attitudes we take toward others. We often imitate those we admire while trying to distinguish ourselves from those who fill us with contempt and disgust. And sometimes we compete with those toward whom we feel envy, including cases in which we envy their virtue. This means that it's important to learn how to feel and express these emotions. In many of his writings, Nietzsche explicitly endeavors to educate his reader's emotional and affective dispositions – yet another form of indirect social influence on the expression of drives calculated to enable agentic and evaluative integration. Indeed, he described his own writing as "a schooling in contempt" (HH "Pref" 1). This is why he sometimes heaps contempt on his targets, such as David Strauss, and venerates virtuous exemplars, such as the character of Zarathustra.

Finally, I turned to the examination of the virtues of one particular type: Nietzsche's own. I argued that he self-attributes two substantive virtues, curiosity and solitude, and two executive virtues, intellectual courage and having a sense of humor. Curiosity and solitude both dispose the agent to engage in inquiry, especially critical inquiry. Whereas curiosity, at least of the Nietzschean variety, motivates inquiry into one's own psychology, including ugly truths about oneself, solitude motivates inquiry into the nature and flaws of one's in-groups, especially one's nonelective in-groups like family, nationality, and so on. It's not hard to see how these drives enjoy agentic integration. Both motivate self-critical inquiry, in one case into the *I*, in the other case into the *we*. Both risk undermining evaluative integration. After all, if I uncover something shameful about myself, I'm liable to then feel shame. Nietzsche's solution is the adoption of courage and having a sense of humor. The courageous inquirer does not fear the answers to hard questions. They enjoy the thrill of overcoming their own psychological resistance. Likewise, having a sense of humor lends a lightness to the inquiry. It enables the curious, solitary inquirer to laugh at herself and her in-group rather than descend into gloomy guilt and shame. Thus, these four Nietzschean virtues are well-suited to both agential and evaluative integration for certain types of people.

These are not the only virtues of the Nietzschean type. He celebrates what he sometimes calls the pathos of distance, which disposes the agent to feel and express appropriate contempt (Alfano 2019). He values a well-tuned sense of prospective shame that lubricates social interaction and enables its bearer to abandon aspects of the self that are not fixed (Alfano 2023a). He thinks that personal style is an expression of the unity of one's virtues (Alfano 2023b). And he holds that, while humility is a vice, intellectual modesty – specifically, the disposition to conduct inquiry using only sufficiently rigorous methods and tools – is a virtue in his type (Alfano 2024).

The self-portrait that Nietzsche paints using the palette of curiosity, solitude, intellectual courage, and having a sense of humor can be attractive. Should you attempt to live a life characterized by these virtues? Should anyone? The answer, if Nietzsche is right about human types, is that it depends. If you find in yourself an insatiable drive to uncover truths, even hard truths, if you can't help but criticize your in-group, if you take delight in overcoming intellectual challenges, and if you gently mock yourself along the way to keep your spirits bright, then these virtues just might be for you. But if not, there is no imperative to cultivate them. The only imperative that Nietzsche has to offer is: become what you are.

Notes on Texts, Translations, and Abbreviations

The following abbreviations and translations of Nietzsche's works are used in this volume.

A *Der Antichrist* (1888); translated as *The Antichrist*. In *The Anti-Christ, Ecce Homo, Twilight of the Idols, and Other Writings*. Edited by A. Ridley & J. Norman. Translated by Judith Norman. Cambridge University Press (2005).

AOM *Vermischte Meinungen und Sprüche* (1879); republished in 1886 in *Menschliches, Allzumenschliches* II); translated as *Assorted Opinions and Maxims*. In *Human, All Too Human*. Translated by R. J. Hollingdale. Cambridge University Press (1986).

BGE *Jenseits von Gut und Böse* (1886): translated as *Beyond Good and Evil*. In *Beyond Good and Evil*. Translated by Judith Norman. Cambridge University Press (2002).

BT *Die Geburt der Tragödie* (1872/1886); translated as *The Birth of Tragedy*. In *The Birth of Tragedy and Other Writings*. Edited by R. Geuss & R. Speirs. Translated by R. Speirs. Cambridge University Press (1999).

CW *Der Fall Wagner* (1888); translated as *The Case of Wagner*. In *The Anti-Christ, Ecce Homo, Twilight of the Idols, and Other Writings*. Edited by A. Ridley & J. Norman. Translated by J. Norman. Cambridge University Press (2005).

D *Morgenröthe* (1881/1887); translated as *Daybreak*. In *Daybreak: Thoughts on the Prejudices of Morality*. Edited by M. Clark & B. Leiter. Translated by R. J. Hollingdale. Cambridge University Press (1997).

DS *David Strauss* (*Unzeitgemässe Betrachtungen* I) (1873); translated as *David Strauss* (*Untimely Meditation* I). In *Untimely Meditations*. Edited by D. Breazeale. Translated by R. J. Hollingdale. Cambridge University Press (1997).

EH *Ecce Homo* (1888); translated as *Ecce Homo*. In *The Anti-Christ, Ecce Homo, Twilight of the Idols, and Other Writings*. Edited by A. Ridley & J. Norman. Translated by Judith Norman. Cambridge University Press (2005).

GM   *Zur Genealogie der Moral* (1887); translated as *On the Genealogy of Morals*. In *On the Genealogy of Morality*. Edited by K. Ansell-Pearson. Translated by C. Diethe. Cambridge University Press (2006).

GS   *Die fröhliche Wissenschaft* (1882/1887); translated as *The Gay Science*. In *The Gay Science: With a Prelude in German Rhymes and an Appendix in Songs*. Edited by B. Williams. Translated by J. Nauckhoff. Cambridge University Press (2001).

HH   *Menschliches, Allzumenschliches* (1878/1886); translated as *Human, All Too Human*. In *Human, All Too Human*. Translated by R. J. Hollingdale. Cambridge University Press (1986).

HL   *Vom Nutzen und Nachteil der Historie für das Leben* (*Unzeitgemässe Betrachtungen* II) (1874); translated as *On the Uses and Disadvantages of History for Life* (*Untimely Meditation* II). In *Untimely Meditations*. Edited by D. Breazeale. Translated by R. J. Hollingdale. Cambridge University Press (1997).

SE   *Schopenhauer als Erzieher* (*Unzeitgemässe Betrachtungen* III) (1874); translated as *Schopenhauer as Educator* (*Untimely Meditation* IV). In *Untimely Meditations*. Edited by D. Breazeale. Translated by R. J. Hollingdale. Cambridge University Press (1997).

TI   *Götzen-Dämmerung* (1888); translated as *Twilight of the Idols*. In *The Anti-Christ, Ecce Homo, Twilight of the Idols, and Other Writings*. Edited by A. Ridley & J. Norman. Translated by Judith Norman. Cambridge University Press (2005).

WS   *Der Wanderer und sein Schatten* (1880; republished in 1886 in *Menschliches, Allzumenschliches* II); translated as *The Wanderer and His Shadow*. In *Human, All Too Human*. Translated by R. J. Hollingdale. Cambridge University Press (1986).

Z   *Also sprach Zarathustra* (1883–1885; part IV was only distributed privately during Nietzsche's lifetime); translated as *Thus Spoke Zarathustra*. In *Thus Spoke Zarathustra: A Book for All and None*. Edited by A. del Caro & R. Pippin. Translated by A. del Caro. Cambridge University Press (2006).

References

Adamson, Peter. (2015). *A History of Philosophy without Any Gaps: Philosophy in the Hellenistic & Roman Worlds*. Oxford University Press.

Alfano, Mark. (2019). *Nietzsche's Moral Psychology*. Cambridge University Press.

Alfano, Mark. (2023a). "The functions of shame in Nietzsche." In R. Rodogno & A. Fussi (eds.), *The Moral Psychology of Shame*, 103–16. Rowman & Littlefield.

Alfano, Mark. (2023b). "Nietzsche on style." *Nineteenth Century Prose*, 50 (1/2): 231–50.

Alfano, Mark. (2024). "Nietzsche on humility and modesty." In J. Steinberg (ed.), *Humility: A History*. Oxford University Press.

Ansell-Pearson, Keith. (1994). *An Introduction to Nietzsche as Political Thinker: The Perfect Nihilist*. Cambridge University Press.

Ansell-Pearson, Keith & Serini, Lorenzo. (2022). "Friedrich Nietzsche: Cheerful thinker and writer. A contribution to the debate on Nietzsche's cheerfulness." *Nietzsche-Studien*, 51(1): 1–33.

Bamford, Rebecca. (2020). "Digital humanities and the history of philosophy: The case of Nietzsche's moral psychology." *Journal of Nietzsche Studies*, 51(2): 241–49.

Berry, Jessica. (2015). "Nietzsche's scientific community: Elective affinities." In J. Young (ed.), *Individual and Community in Nietzsche's Philosophy*, 93–117. Cambridge University Press.

Creasy, Kaitlyn. (2020). *The Problem of Affective Nihilism in Nietzsche*. Springer International.

Cristy, Rachel. (2019). "'Being just is always a positive attitude': Justice in Nietzsche's virtue epistemology." *Journal of Nietzsche Studies*, 50(1): 33–57.

Cristy, Rachel. (2020). "Virtue and community in Mark Alfano's *Nietzsche's Moral Psychology*." *Journal of Nietzsche Studies*, 51(2): 250–55.

Gemes, Ken. (2009). "Freud and Nietzsche on sublimation." *Journal of Nietzsche Studies*, 38: 38–59.

Gemes, Ken. (2013). "Life's perspectives." In K. Gemes & J. Richardson (eds.), *The Oxford Handbook of Nietzsche*, 553–75. Oxford University Press.

Gordon, Mordechai. (2016). "Camus, Nietzsche, and the absurd: Rebellion and scorn versus humor and laughter." *Philosophy and Literature*, 39(2): 364–78.

Harper, Aaron. (2015). "Nietzsche's thumbscrew: Honesty as virtue and value standard." *Journal of Nietzsche Studies*, 46(3): 367–90.

Hatab, Lawrence. (1988). "Laughter in Nietzsche's thought." *International Studies in Philosophy*, 20(2): 67–79.

Higgins, Kathleen. (1994). *On the Genealogy of Morals* — Nietzsche's *gift*. In R. Schacht (ed.), *Nietzsche, Genealogy, Morality: Essays on Nietzsche's Genealogy Morals*, 49–62. University of California Press,

Higgins, Kathleen. (2000). *Comic Relief: Nietzsche's Gay Science*. Oxford University Press.

Huddleston, Andrew. (2014). "'Consecration to culture': Nietzsche on slavery and human dignity." *Journal of the History of Philosophy*, 52(1): 135–60.

Huddleston, Andrew. (2017). "Nietzsche on the health of the soul." *Inquiry*, 60 (1–2): 135–64.

Huddleston, Andrew. (2019). *Nietzsche on the Decadence and Flourishing of Culture*. Oxford University Press.

Hunt, Lester. (1993). *Nietzsche and the Origins of Virtue*. Routledge.

Hurka, Thomas. (2007). "Nietzsche: Perfectionist." In B. Leiter & N. Sinhababu (eds.), *Nietzsche and Morality*, 9–31. Oxford University Press.

Janaway, Christopher. (2007). *Beyond Selflessness: Reading Nietzsche's "Genealogy."* Oxford University Press.

Jenkins, Scott. (2016). "Truthfulness as Nietzsche's highest virtue." *Journal of Value Inquiry*, 50(1): 1–19.

Katsafanas, Paul. (2011a). "The concept of unified agency in Nietzsche, Plato, and Schiller." *Journal of the History of Philosophy*, 49(1): 87–113.

Katsafanas, Paul. (2011b). "Deriving ethics from action: A Nietzschean version of constitutivism." *Philosophy and Phenomenological Research*, 83(3): 620–60.

Katsafanas, Paul. (2013). "Nietzsche's philosophical psychology." In J. Richardson & K. Gemes (eds.), *Oxford Handbook of Nietzsche*, 727–55. Oxford University Press.

Katsafanas, Paul. (2016). *The Nietzschean Self: Moral Psychology, Agency, and the Unconscious*. Oxford University Press.

Kaufmann, Walter. (1968). *Nietzsche: Philosopher, Psychologist, Antichrist*. Vintage Books.

Kuehne, Tobias. (2018). "Nietzsche's ethics of danger." *Journal of Nietzsche Studies*, 49(1): 78–101.

Leiter, Brian. (2002). *Nietzsche on Morality*. Routledge.

Lippitt, John. (1992). "Nietzsche, Zarathustra, and the status of laughter." *British Journal of Aesthetics*, 32(1): 39–49.

Magnus, Bernd. (1980). "Aristotle and Nietzsche: 'Megalopsychia' and 'uebermensch'." In D. Depew (ed.), *The Greeks and the Good Life*, 260–95. California State University Press.

May, Simon. (1999). *Nietzsche's Ethics and His War on "Morality."* Oxford University Press.

Miyasaki, Donovan. (2022). *Nietzsche's Immoralism: Politics as First Philosophy*. Springer.

More, Nicholas. (2014). *Nietzsche's Last Laugh: Ecce Homo as Satire*. Cambridge University Press.

Morreall, John. (1983). *Taking Laughter Seriously*. SUNY Press.

Pappas, Nicholas. (2005). "Morality gags." *The Monist*, 88(1): 52–71.

Pichler, Alex & Reiter, Nils. (2022). "From concepts to texts and back: Operationalization as a core activity of digital humanities." *Journal of Cultural Analytics*, 7(4). https://culturalanalytics.org/article/57195-from-con cepts-to-texts-and-back-operationalization-as-a-core-activity-of-digital-humanities.

Reginster, Bernard. (2006). *The Affirmation of Life*. Cambridge University Press.

Reginster, Bernard. (2013). "Honesty and curiosity in Nietzsche's free spirit." *Journal of the History of Philosophy*, 55(3): 441–63.

Reginster, Bernard. (2015). "Nietzsche, proficiency, and the (new) spirit of capitalism." *Journal of Value Inquiry*, 49: 453–77.

Reginster, Bernard. (2020). "Comments on Mark Alfano's *Nietzsche's Moral Psychology*." *Journal of Nietzsche Studies*, 51(2): 256–64.

Riccardi, Mattia. (2021). *Nietzsche's Philosophical Psychology*. Oxford University Press.

Richardson, John. (1996). *Nietzsche's System*. Oxford University Press.

Richardson, John. (2015). "Nietzsche, language, and community." In J. Young (ed.), *Individual and Community in Nietzsche's Philosophy*, 214–44. Cambridge University Press.

Snelson, Avery. (2017). "Nietzsche on the origin of conscience and obligation." *The Journal of Nietzsche Studies*, 50(2): 310–31.

Swanton, Christine. (2015). *The Virtue Ethics of Hume & Nietzsche*. Wiley Blackwell.

Turri, John. (2015). "Unreliable knowledge." *Philosophy and Phenomenological Research*, 90(3): 529–45.

Watson, Lani. (2018). "Curiosity and inquisitiveness." In H. Battaly (ed.), *Handbook of Virtue Epistemology*, 155–66. Routledge.

Weeks, Mark. (2004). "Beyond a joke: Nietzsche and the birth of 'super-laughter'." *Journal of Nietzsche Studies*, 27(1): 1–17.

White, Alan. (2001). "The youngest virtue." In R. Schacht (ed.), *Nietzsche's Post-Moralism*, 63–78. Cambridge University Press.

Wirth, Jason. (2005). "Nietzsche's joy: On laughter's truth." *Epoché*, 10(1): 117–39.

Acknowledgments

I started my first book on Nietzsche in 2013 and finished it in 2019. It represents my effort, over those years, to come to grips with his moral psychology, including his evolving conceptions of virtue and character as they relate to one's community. It was perhaps too ambitious, attempting to articulate a complete theory and illustrate it with examples from the earliest to the latest works. This Element, which was composed in August 2023, has a more modest aim: to concisely outline Nietzsche's conception of virtue in his middle, mature, and late works, without any pretension to comprehensiveness.

I have benefited from feedback on my prior work from attendees to talks I've given at Tilburg University, CUNY, Wollongong University, Utrecht University, University of Genoa, Guelph University, UNC-Chapel Hill, the APA in New Orleans, University of Lisbon, Groningen University, the AAP in Melbourne, Kaunas Technical University, Birkbeck University, and Western Washington University. I have also benefited from comments from anonymous referees for various journals and post-publication reviews by Mattia Riccardi, Neil Sinhababu, Rebecca Bamford, Rachel Cristy, Bernard Reginster, Paul Katsafanas, and Kaitlyn Creasy. And I have benefited from technical support in corpus analysis from my friend and collaborator Marc Cheong. In the last couple of years, I have also learned a great deal about virtue from my friend and collaborator Mandi Astola, who has also done much-appreciated service to the discipline. The current Element reflects the extent to which I have managed to learn more from Nietzsche's writings and digest my colleagues' insights. I hope that the result is a less long-winded and more coherent account of his understanding of virtue.

I would be remiss if I did not acknowledge the institutional support that made it possible for me to do this work. I am grateful to Macquarie University, especially the philosophy department, and most especially to Richard Menary, who almost single-handedly managed to evacuate me from pandemic-stricken Europe to Australia in 2020. I continue to be surprised by just how smart, competent, and kind my colleagues are. They make it easier to embrace *amor fati*.

For Mandi

Philosophy of Friedrich Nietzsche

Kaitlyn Creasy

California State University, San Bernardino

Kaitlyn Creasy is Associate Professor of Philosophy at California State University, San Bernardino. She is the author of *The Problem of Affective Nihilism in Nietzsche* (2020) as well as several articles in nineteenth-century philosophy and moral psychology.

Matthew Meyer

The University of Scranton

Matthew Meyer is Professor of Philosophy at the University of Scranton. He is the author of three monographs: *Reading Nietzsche through the Ancients: An Analysis of Becoming, Perspectivism, and The Principle of Non-Contradiction* (2014), *Nietzsche's Free Spirit Works: A Dialectical Reading* (Cambridge, 2019), and *The Routledge Guidebook to Thus Spoke Zarathustra* (2024). He has also co-edited, with Paul Loeb, *Nietzsche's Metaphilosophy: The Nature, Method, and Aims of Philosophy* (Cambridge, 2019).

About the Series

Friedrich Nietzsche is one of the most important and influential philosophers of the nineteenth century. This Cambridge Elements series offers concise and structured overviews of a range of central topics in his thought, written by a diverse group of experts with a variety of approaches.

Cambridge Elements ☰

Philosophy of Friedrich Nietzsche

Elements in the Series

A full series listing is available at: www.cambridge.org/EPFN